TIME TO COLOR

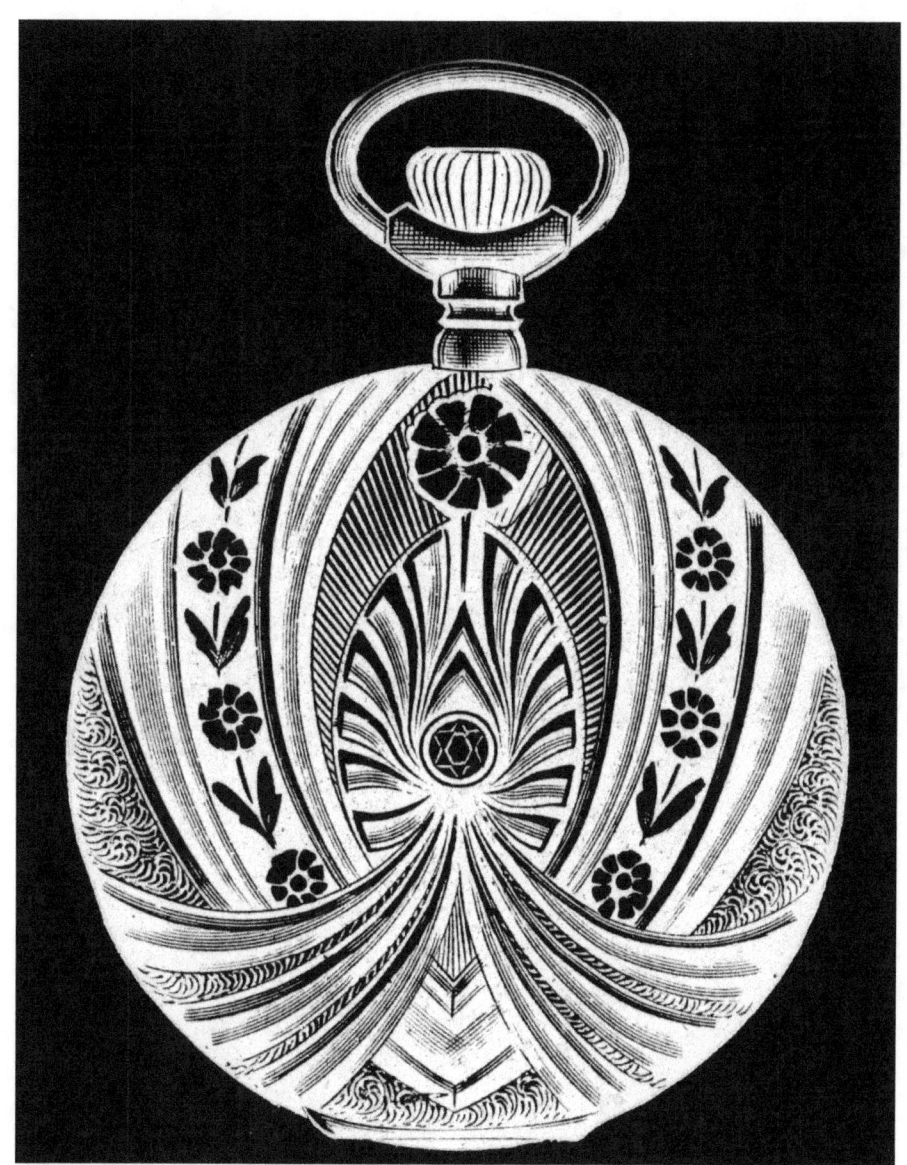

GRAYSCALE ADULT COLORING BOOK OF ANTIQUE POCKET WATCH PATTERNS

OLDE GLORIE STUDIOS

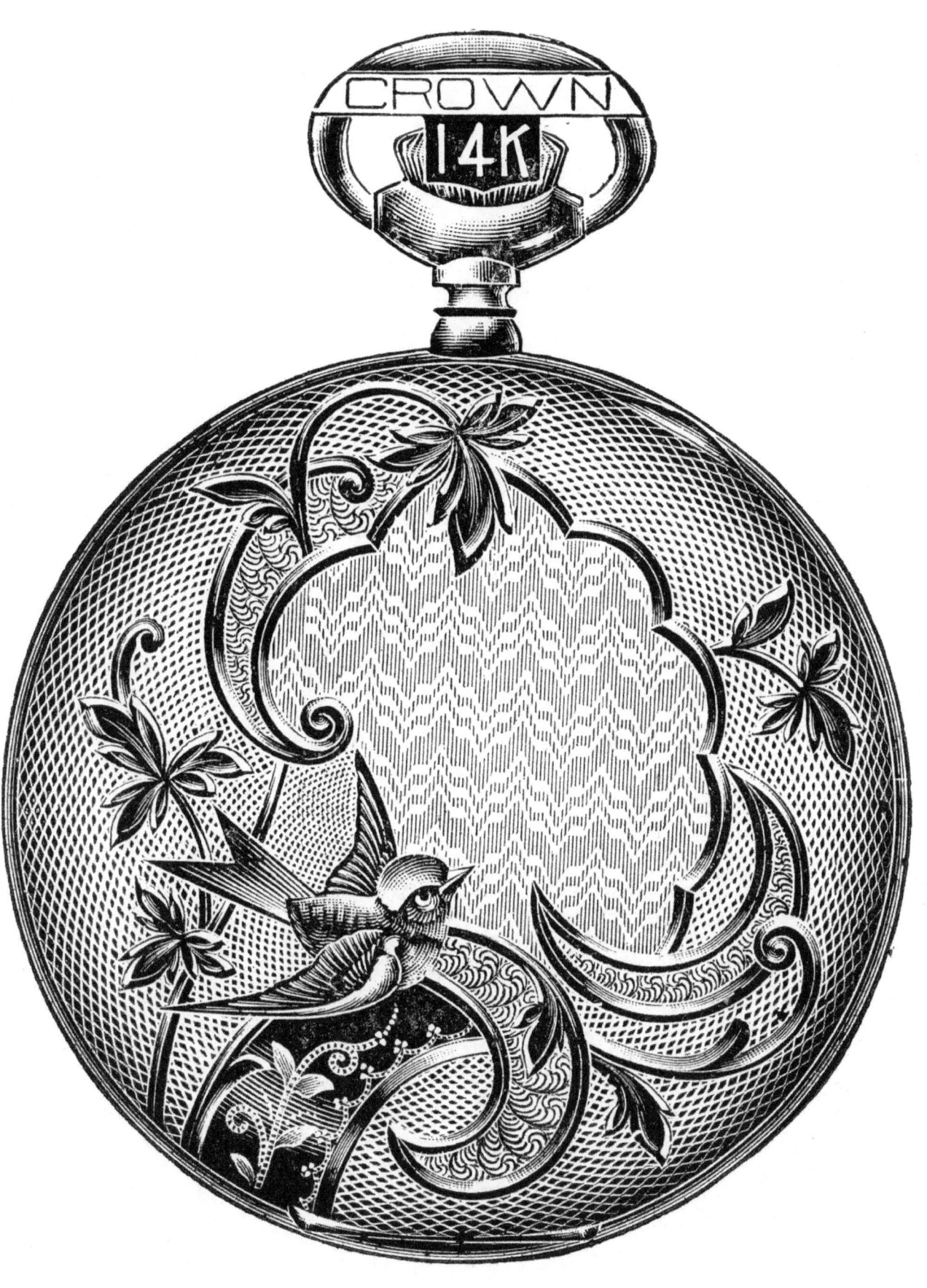

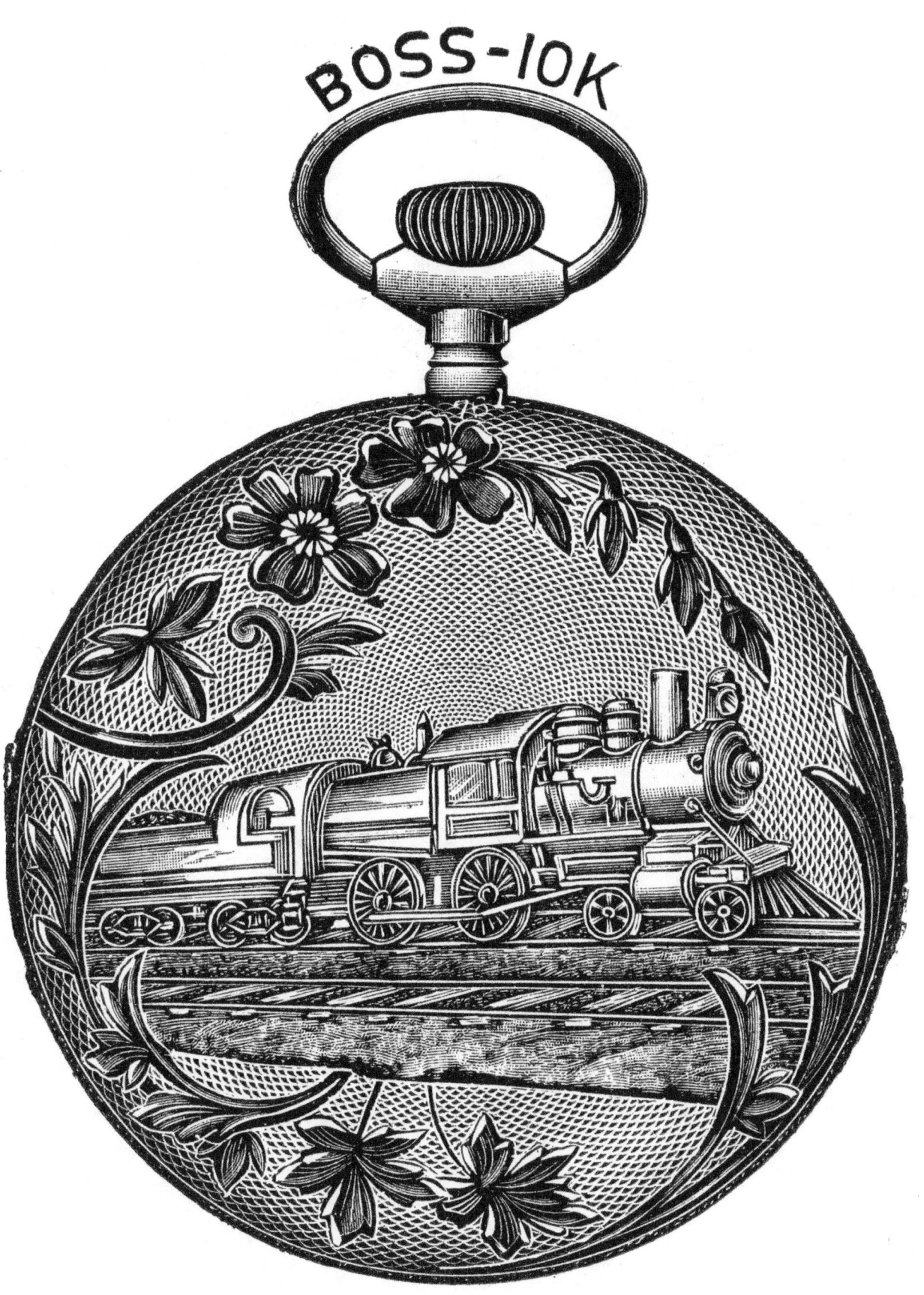

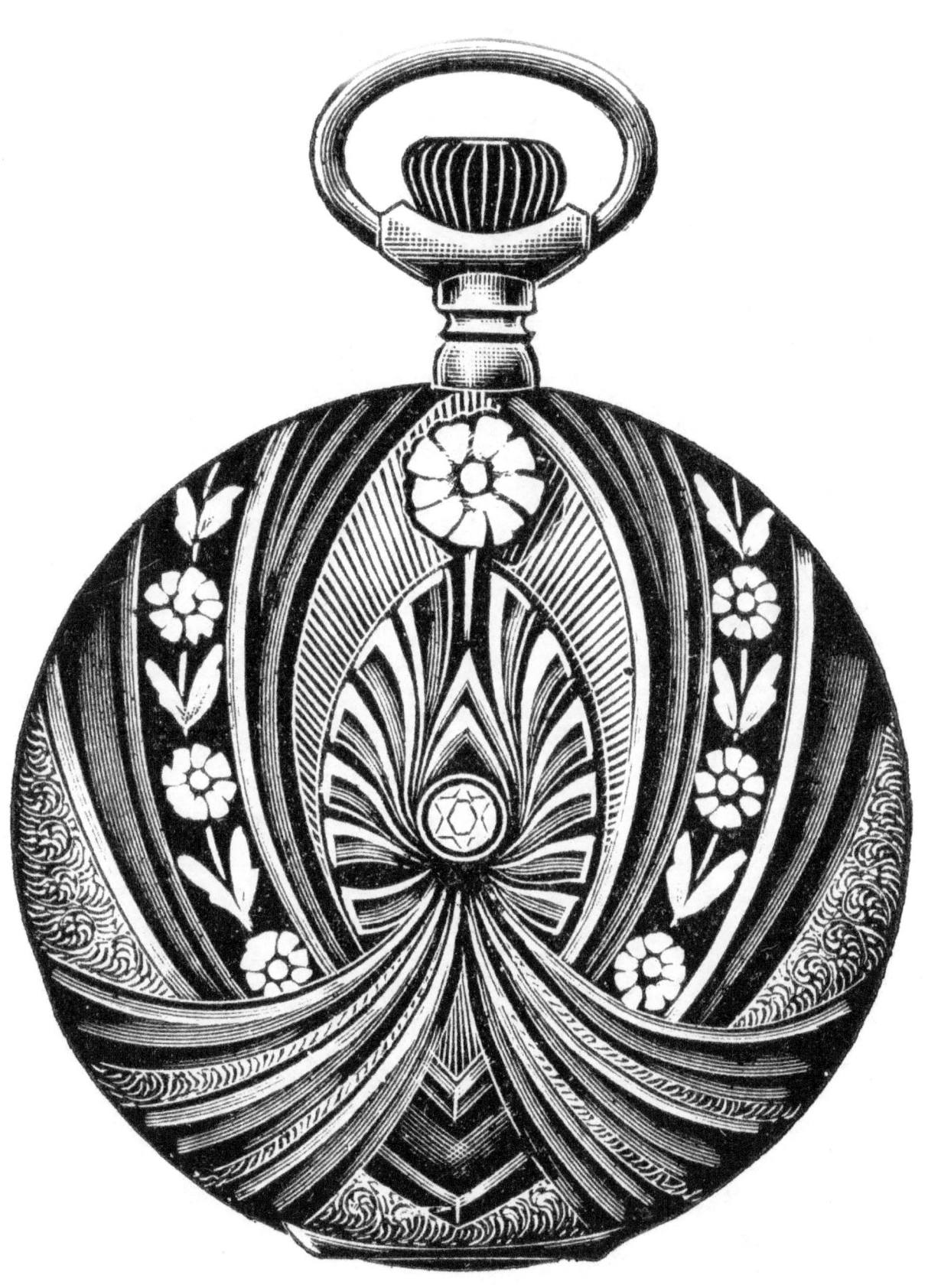

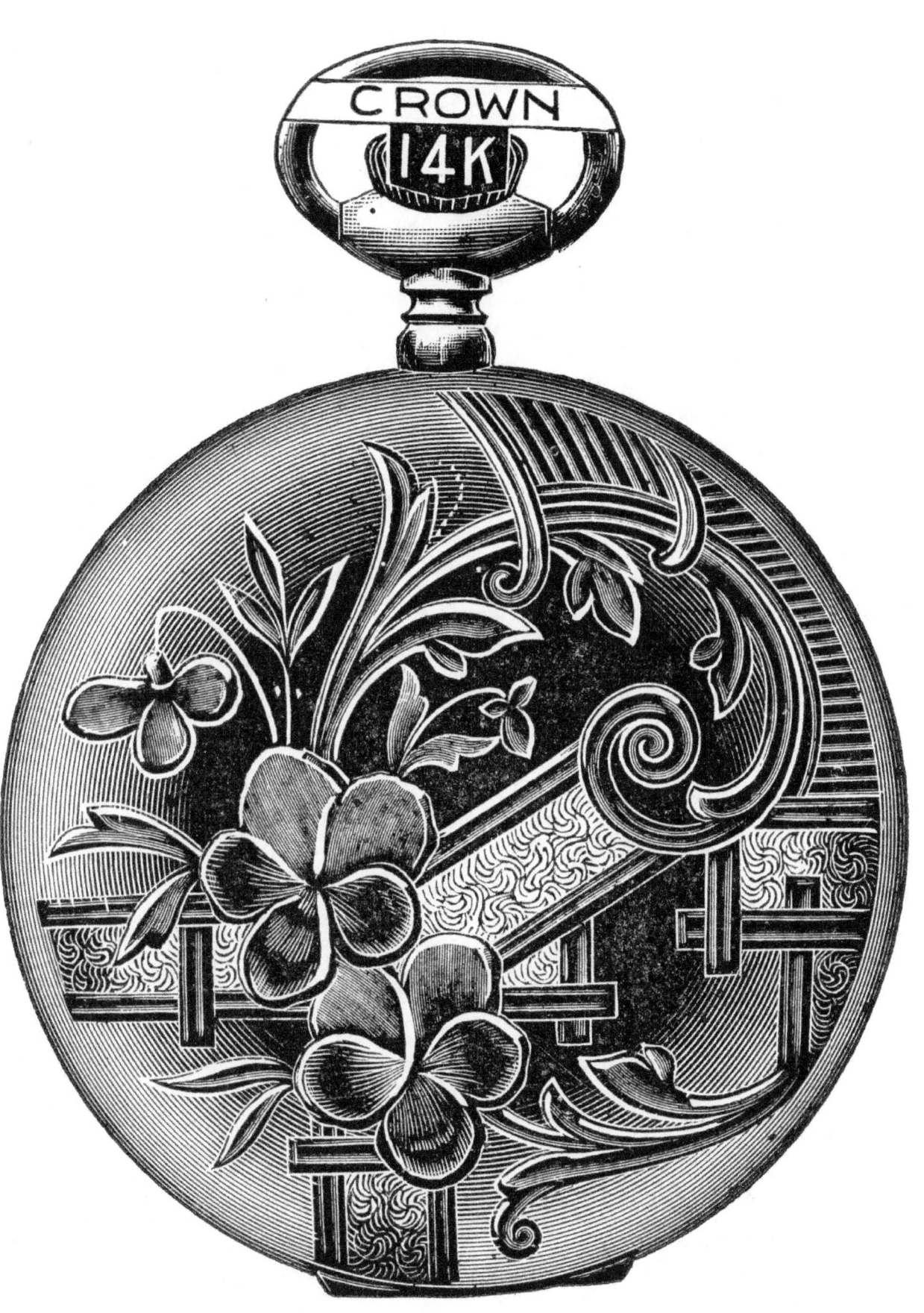

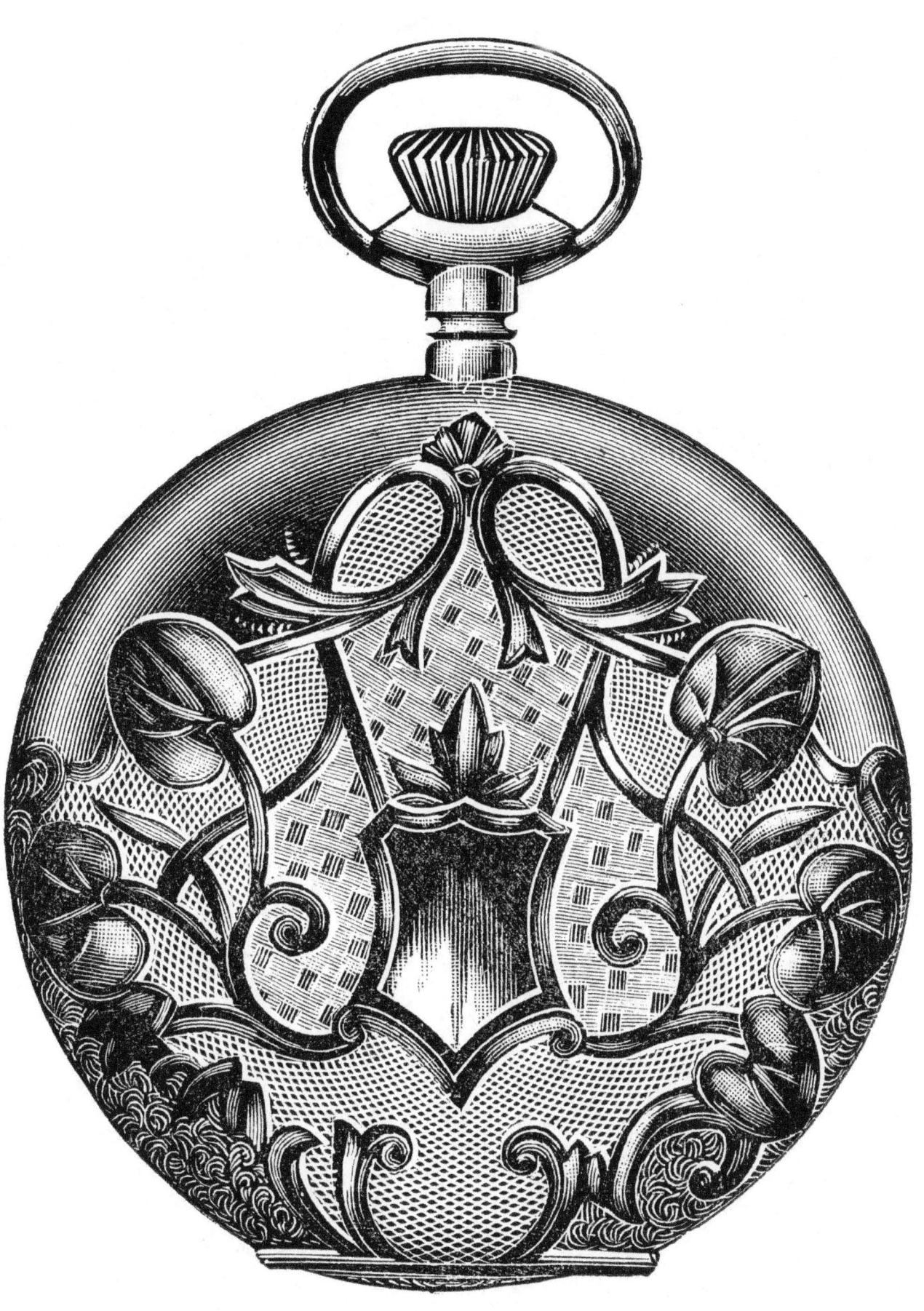

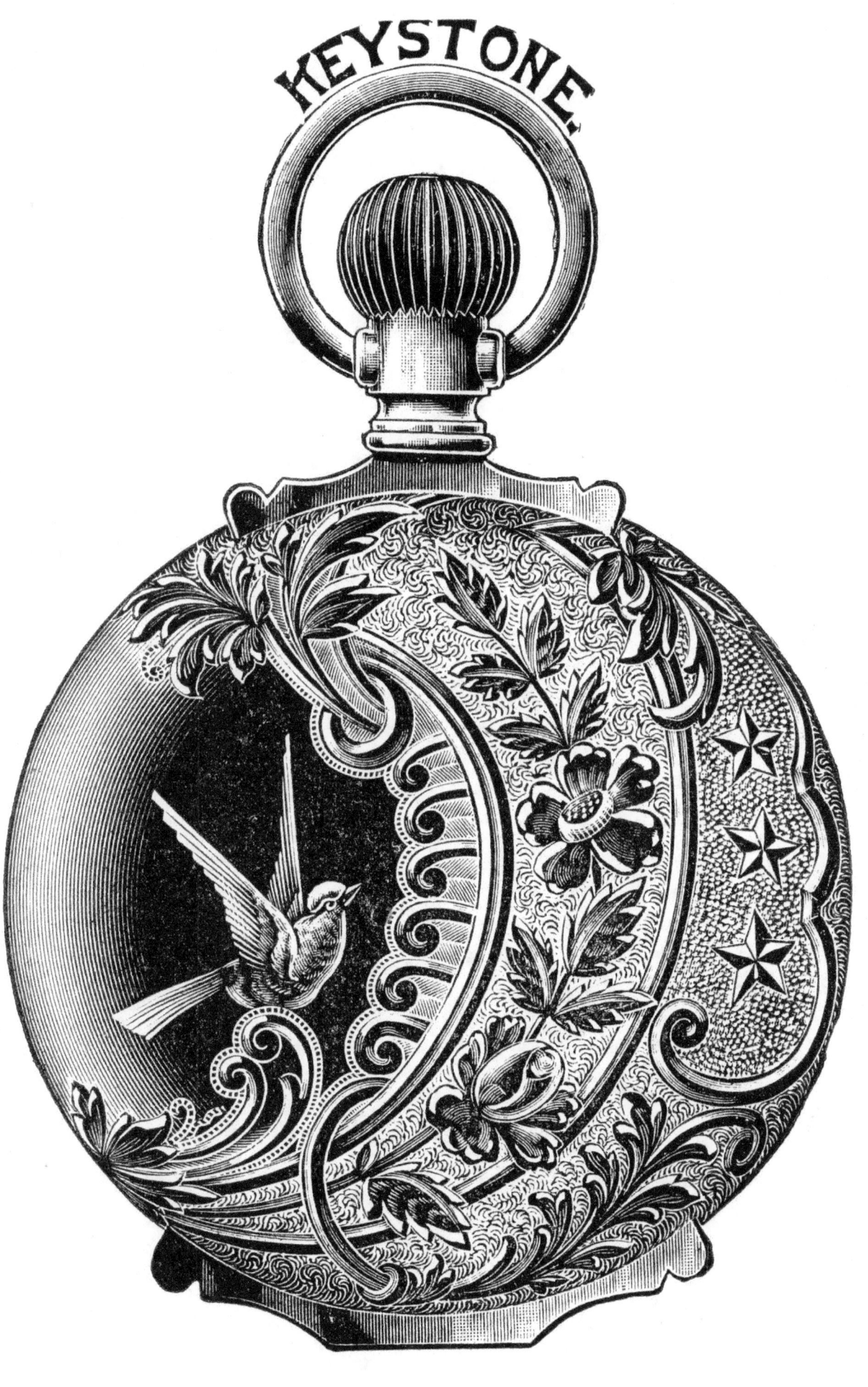

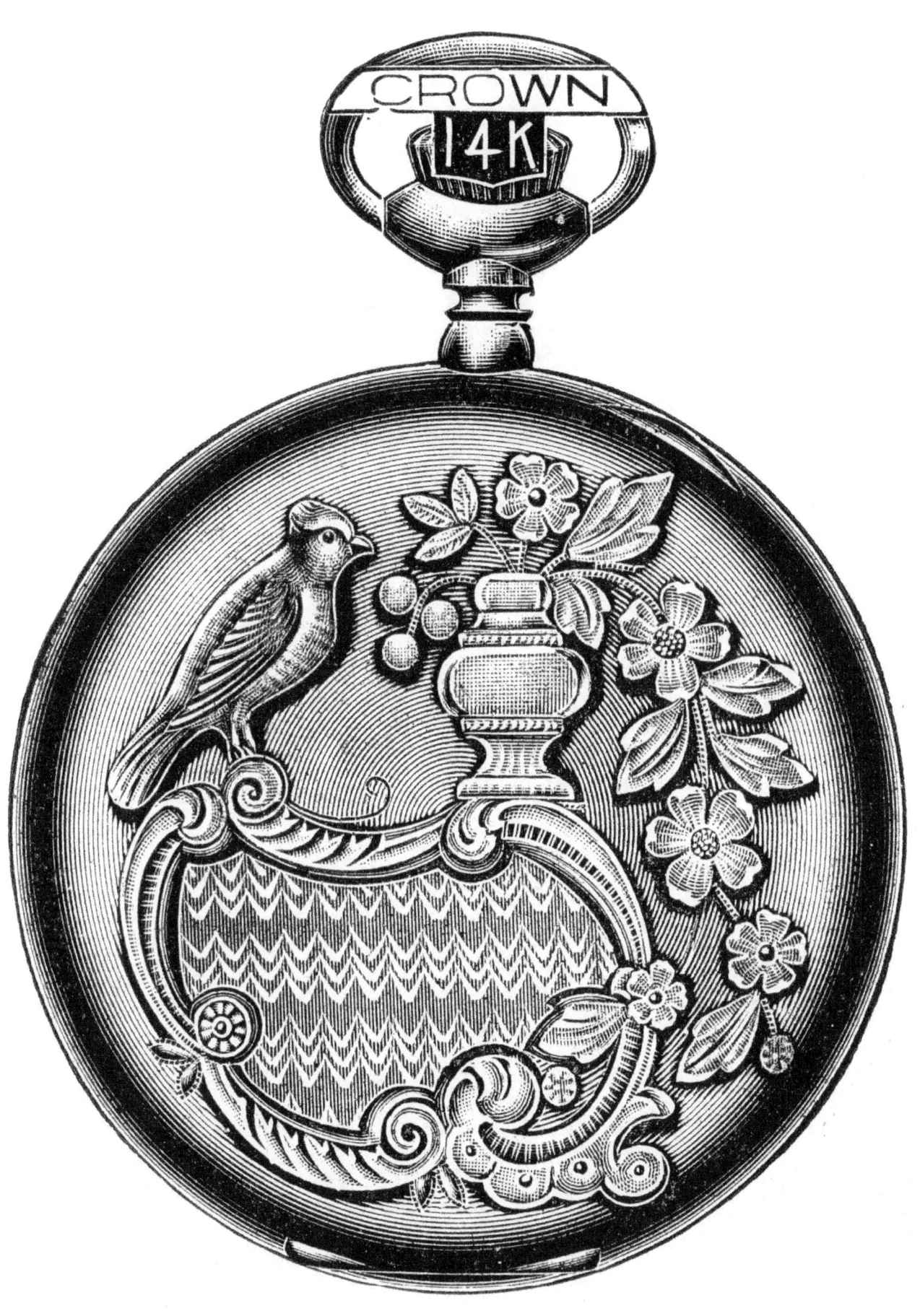

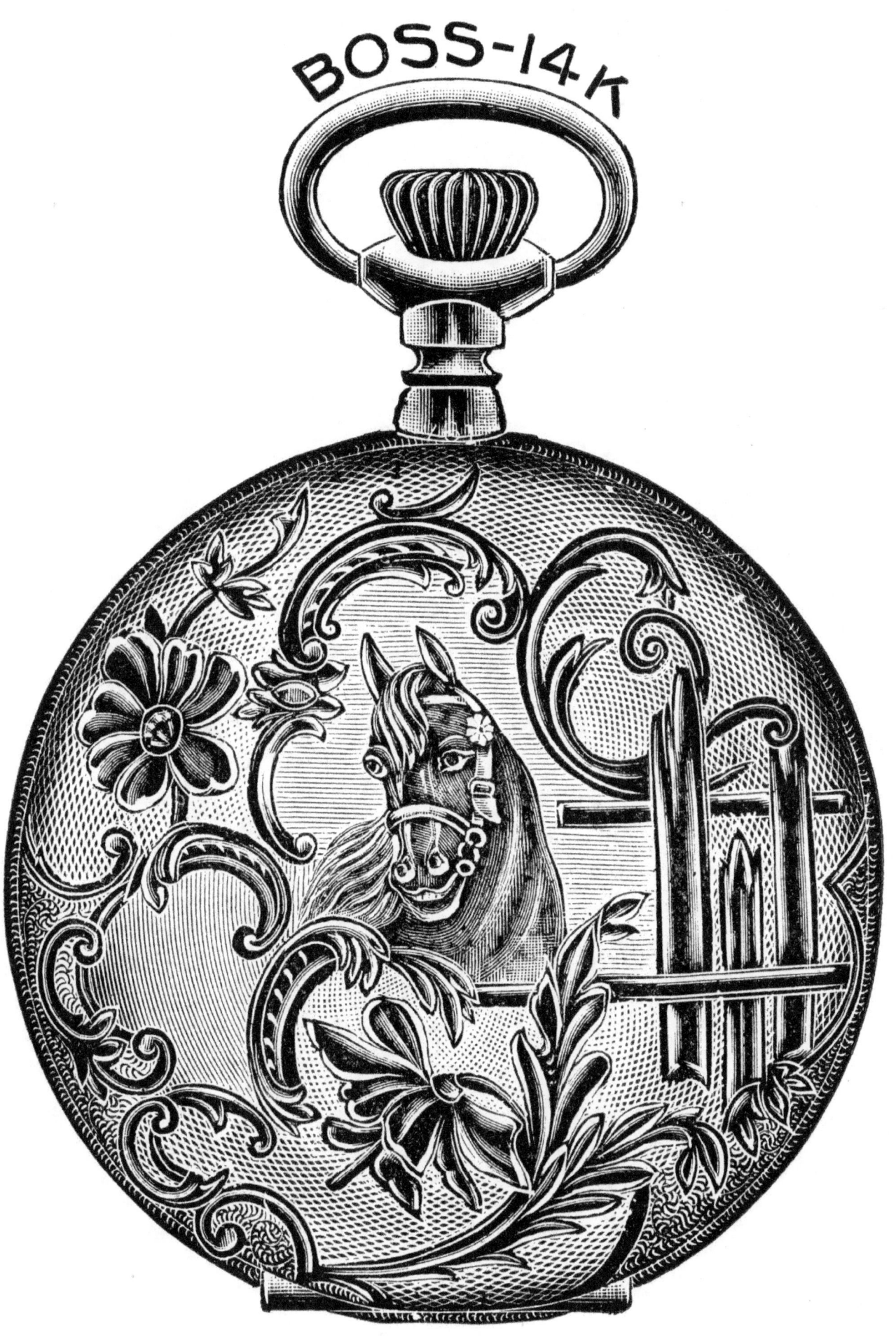

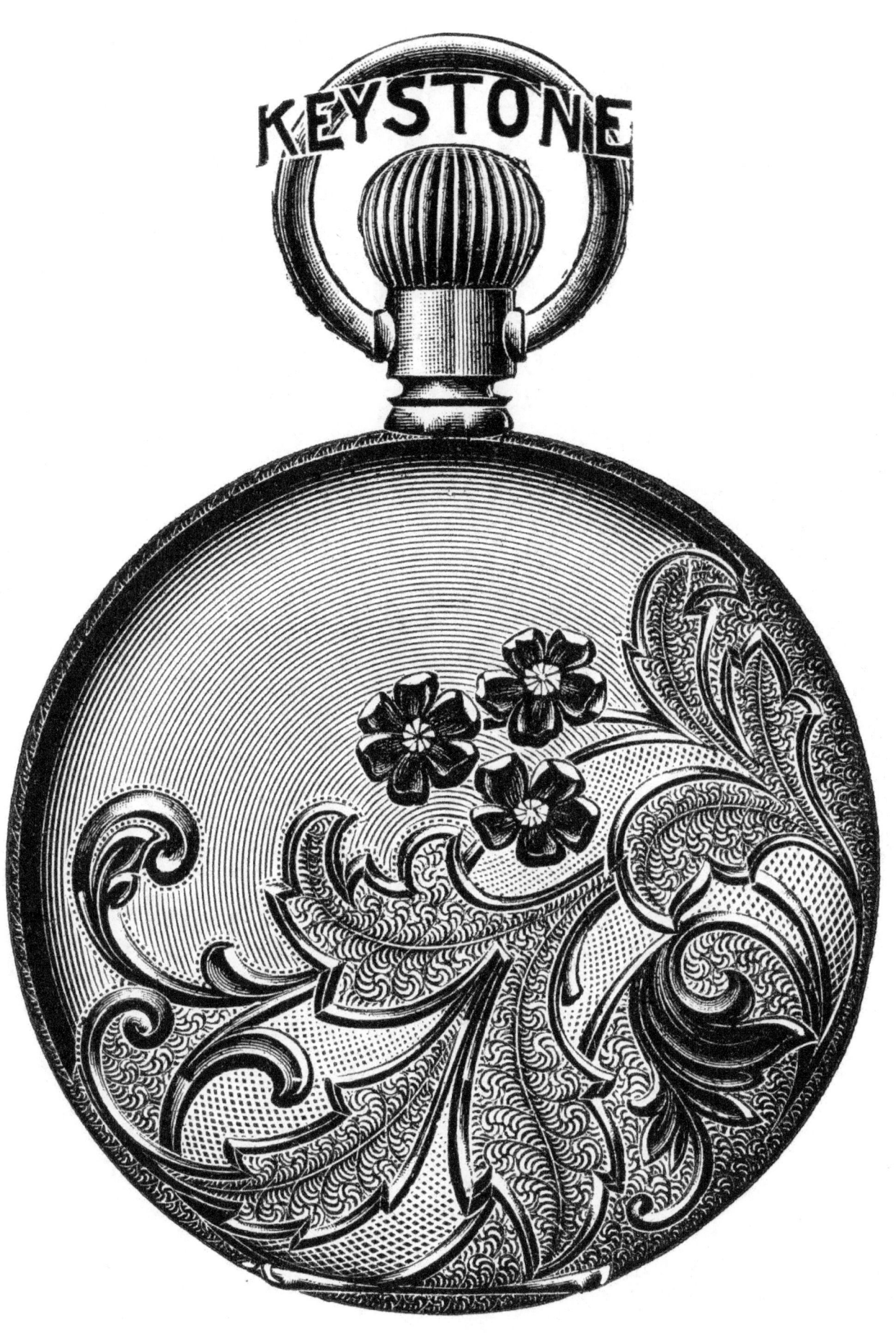

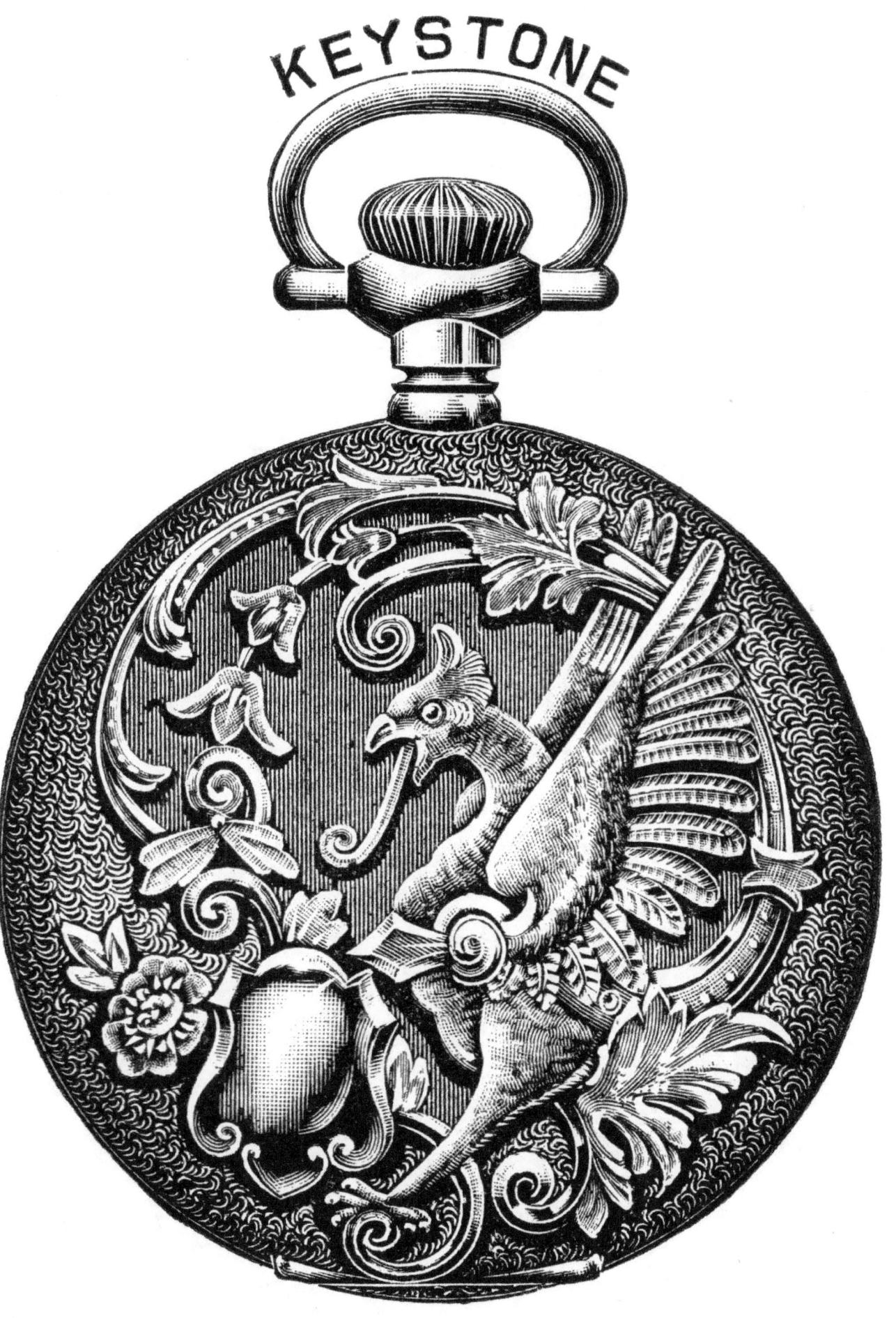

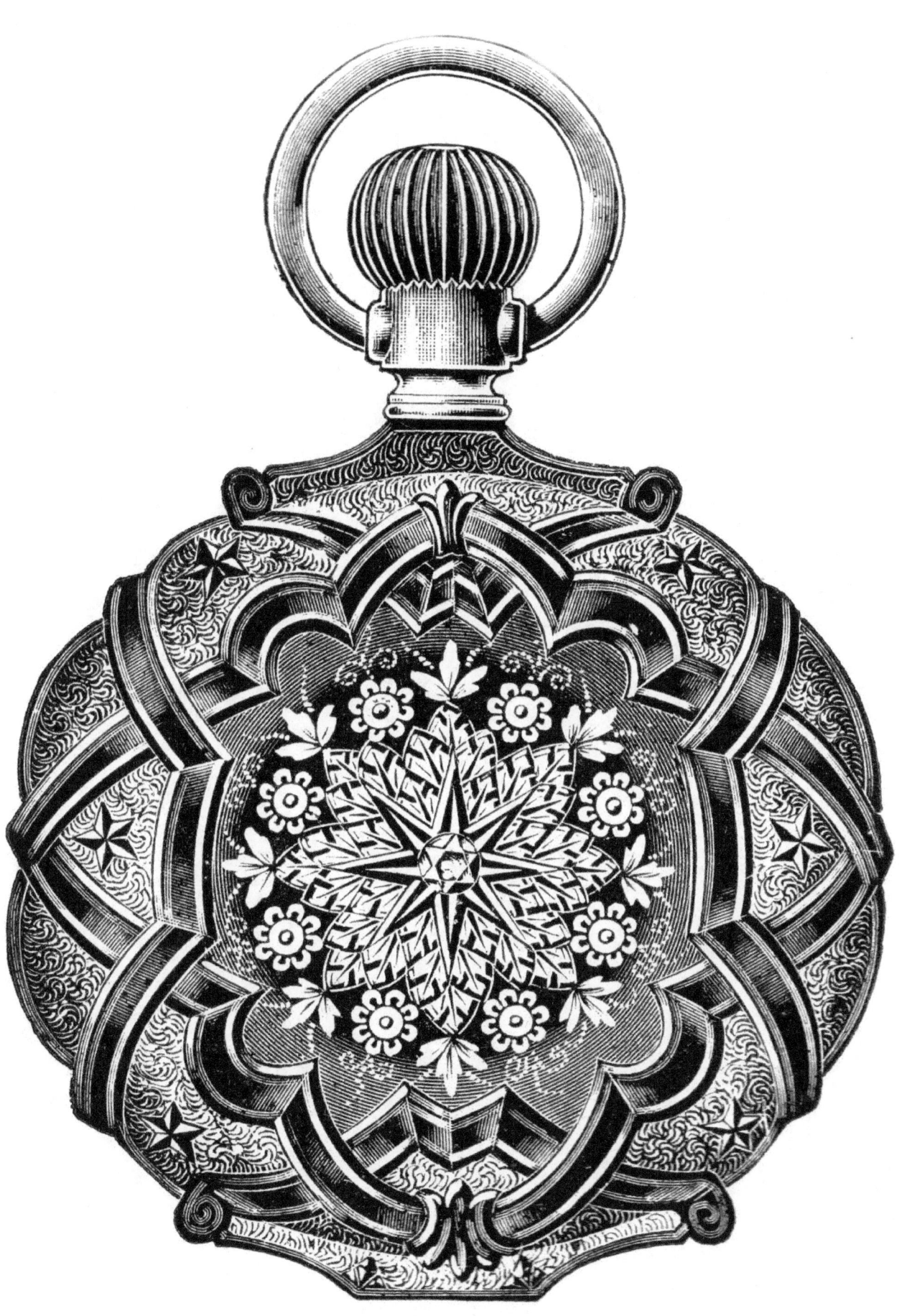

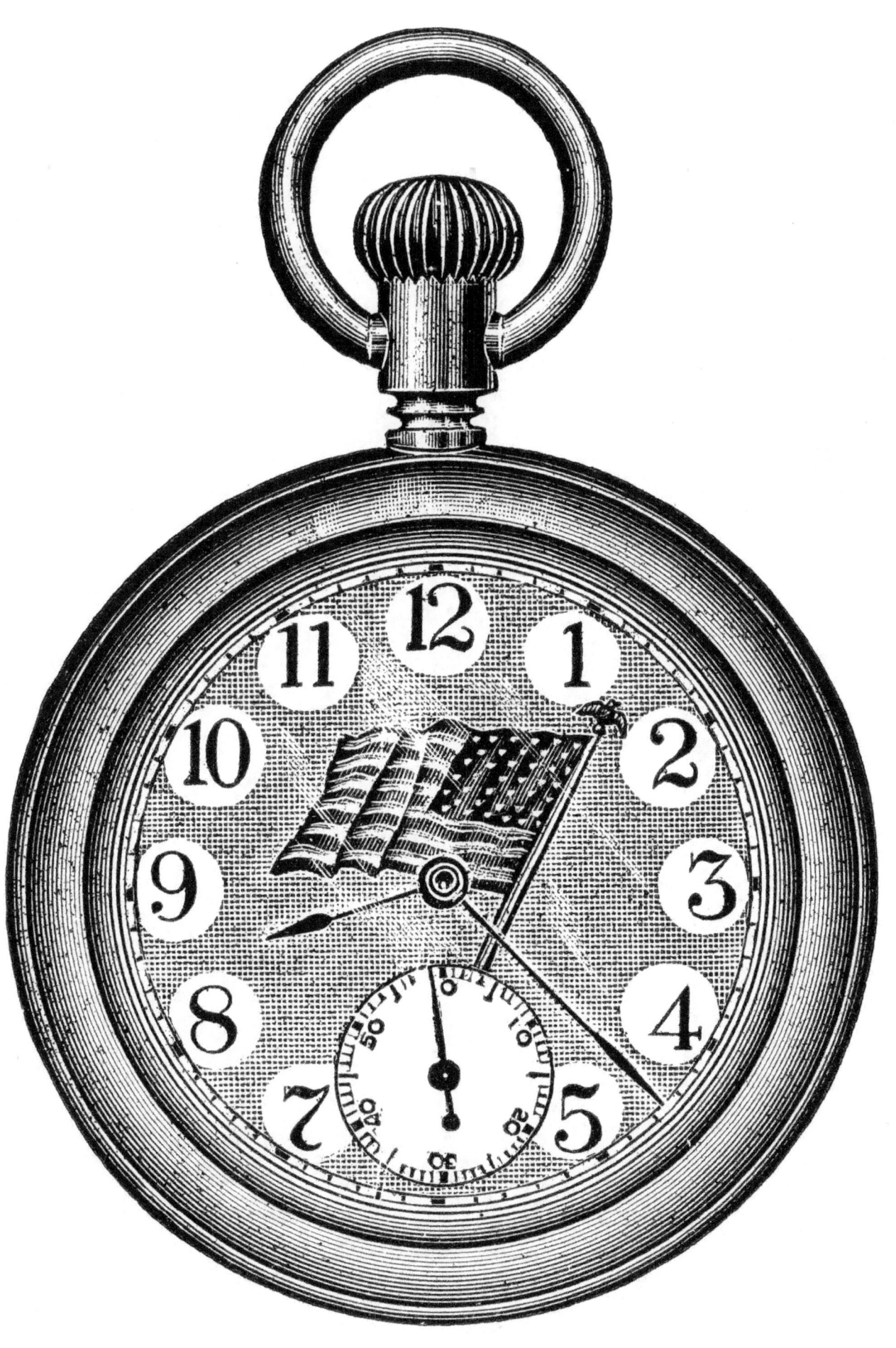

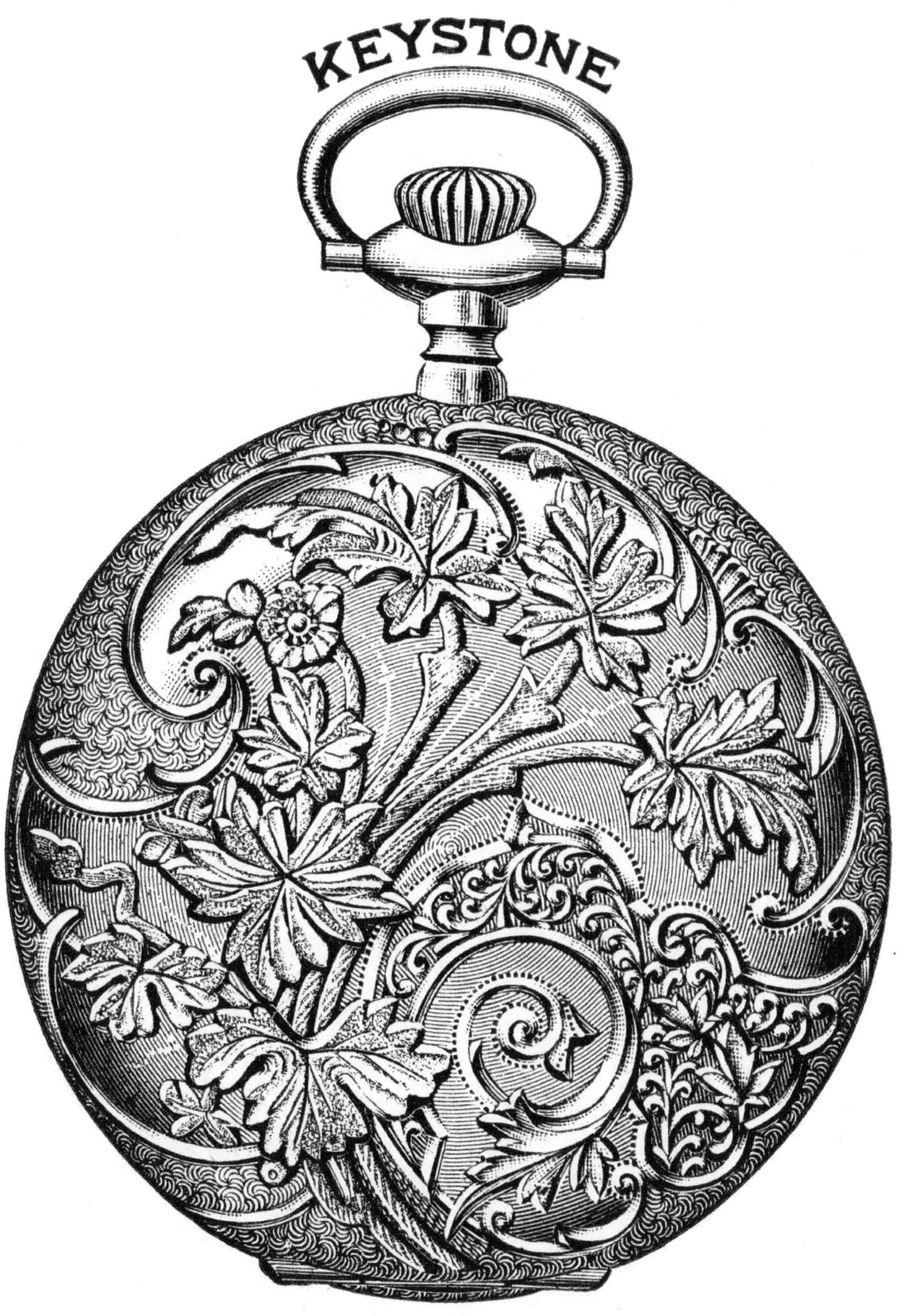

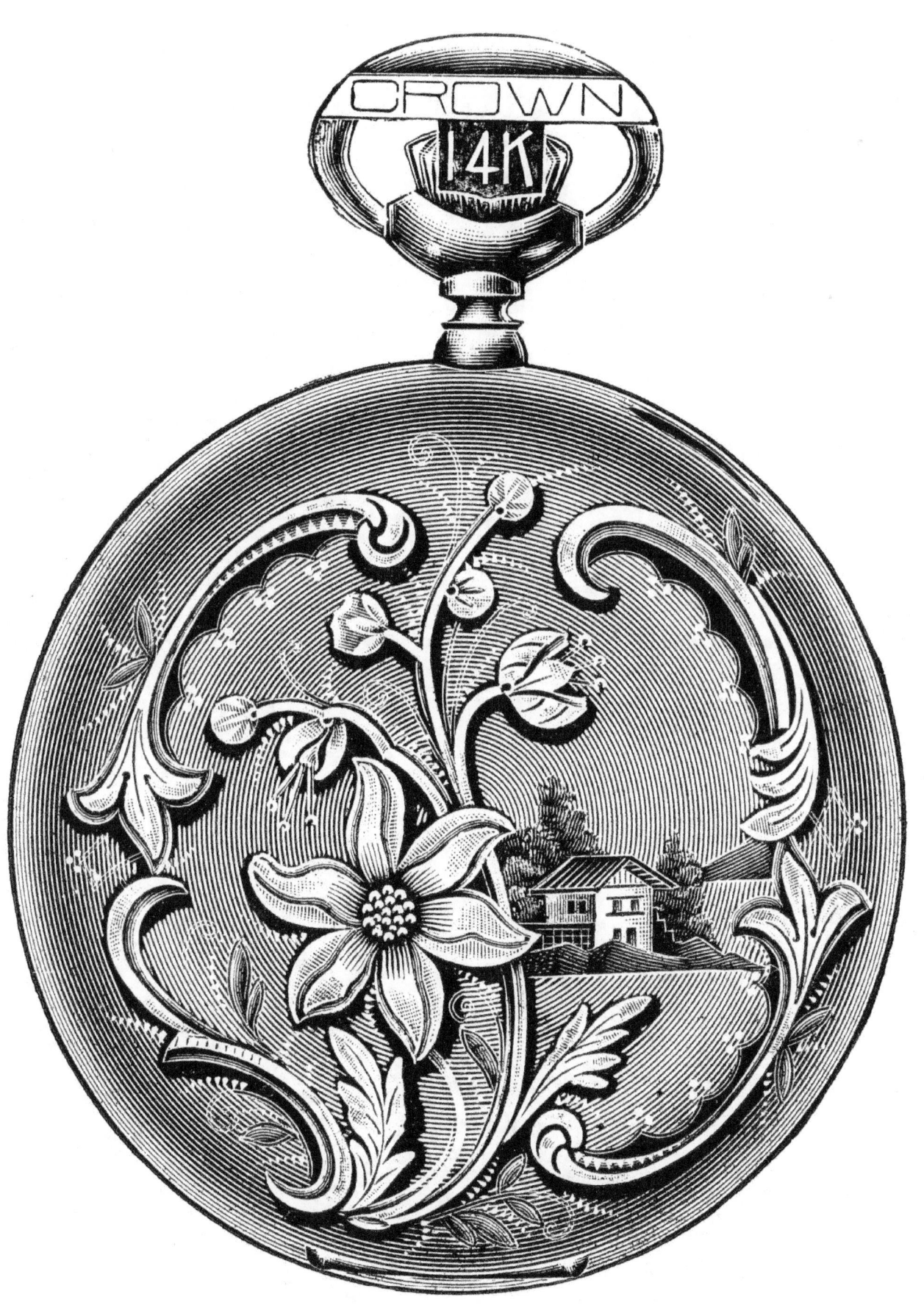

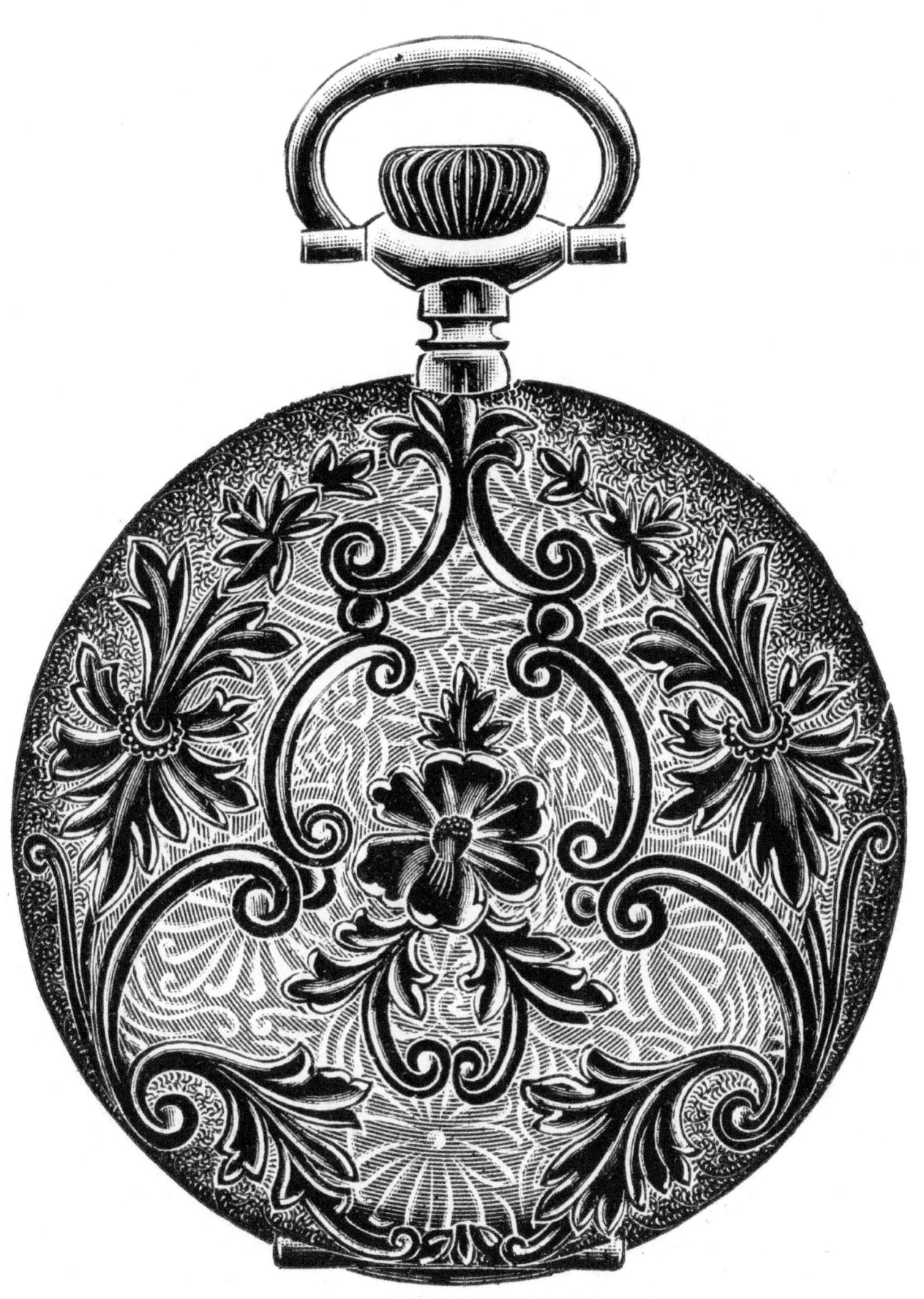

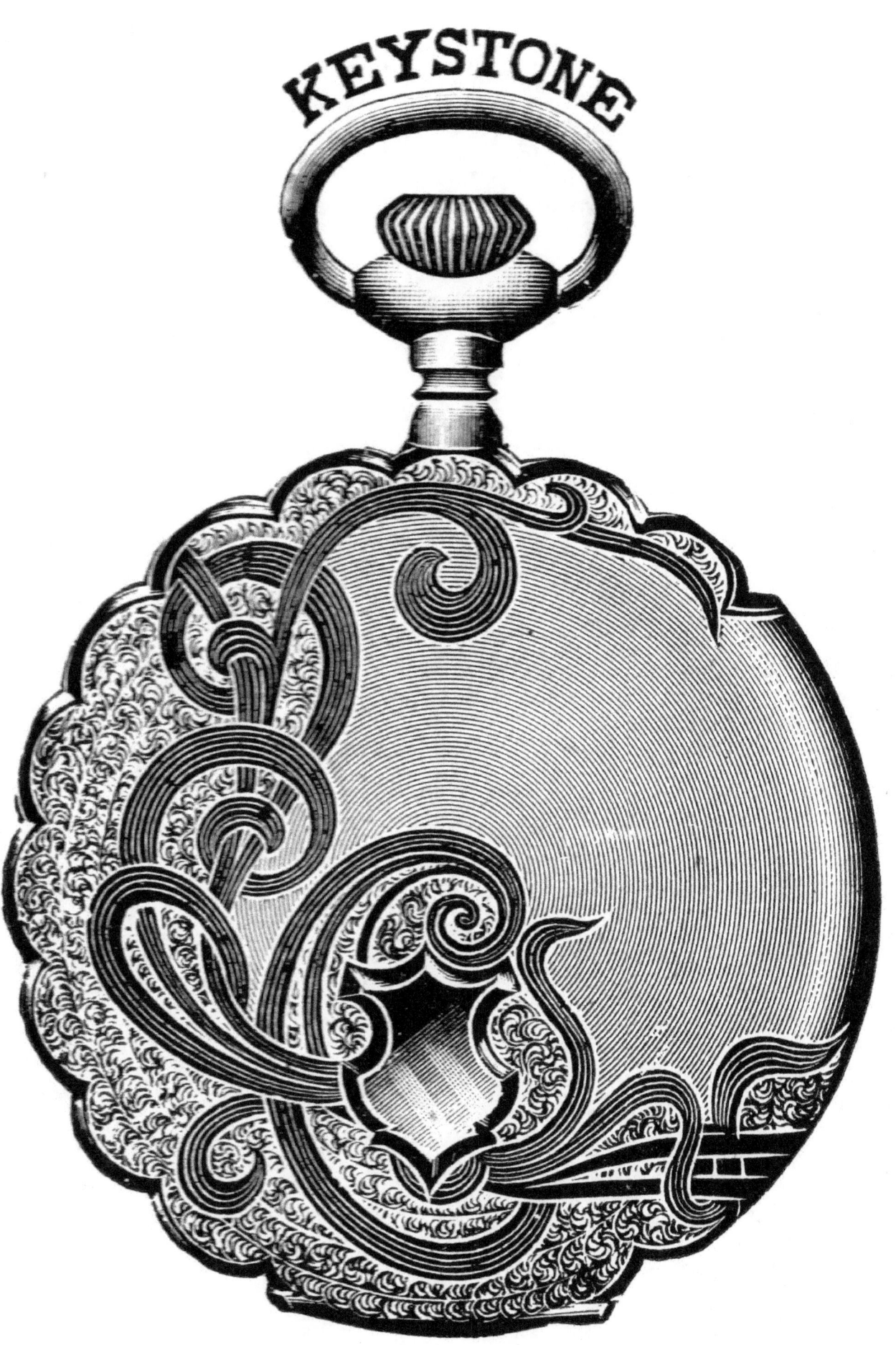

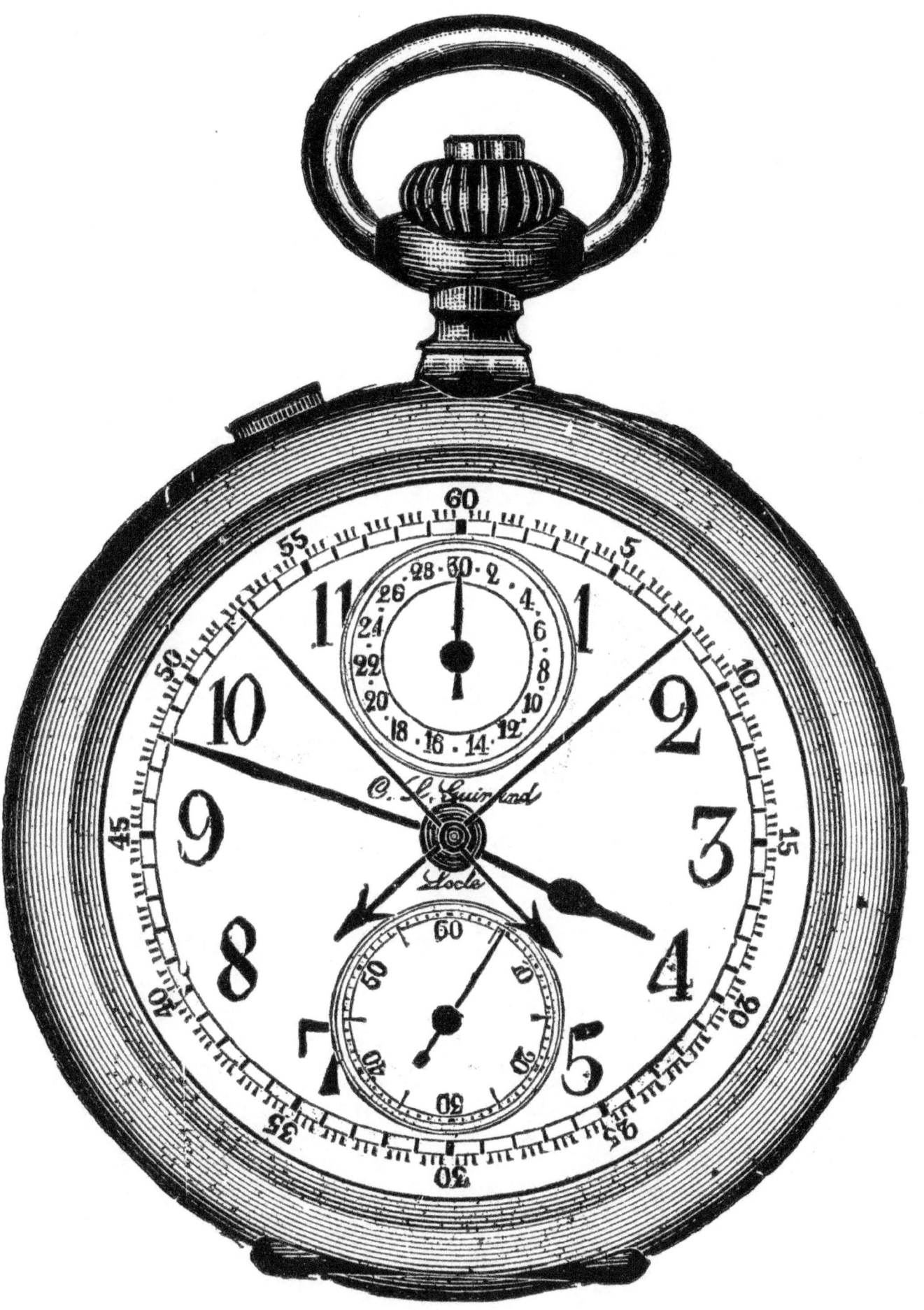

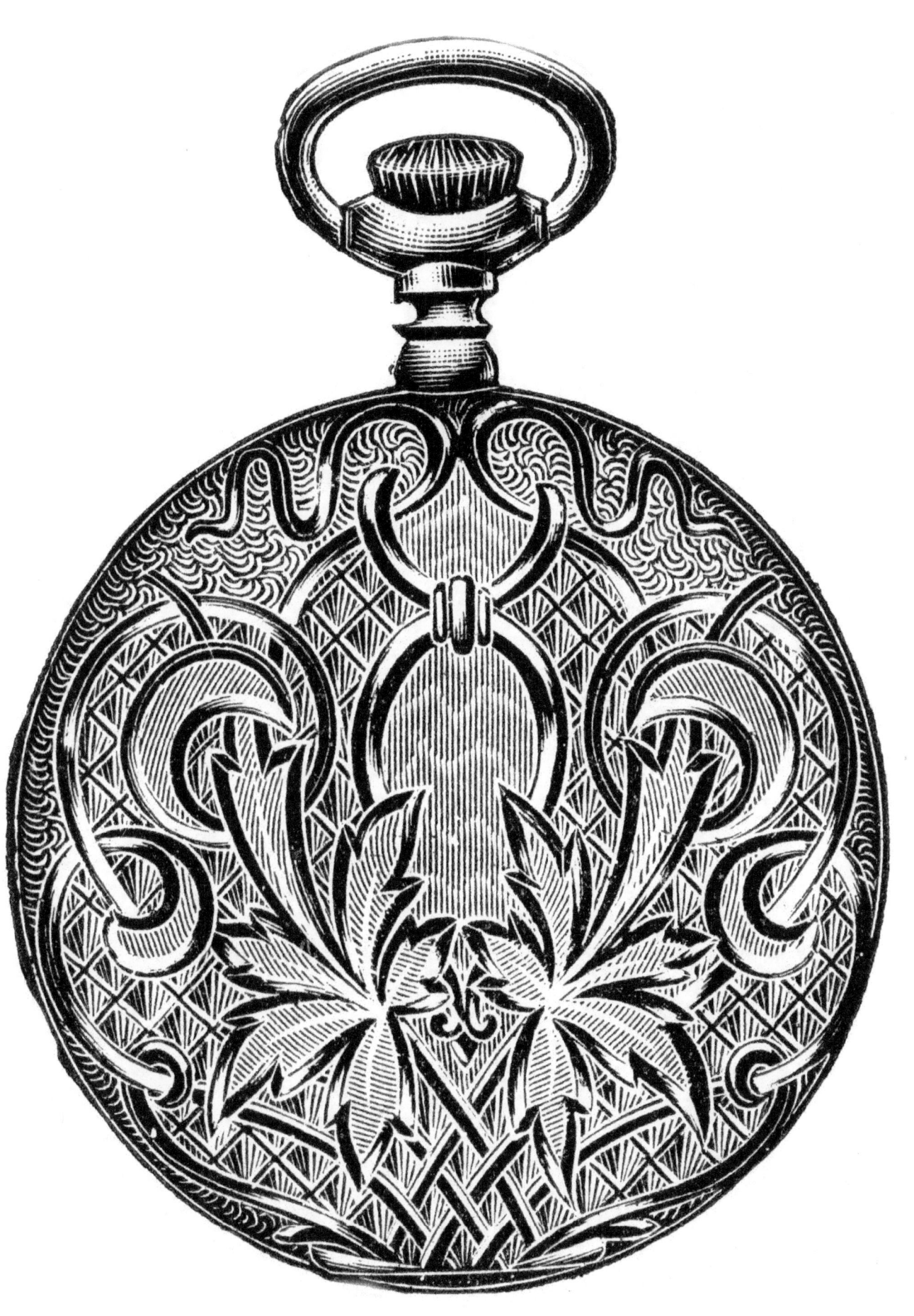

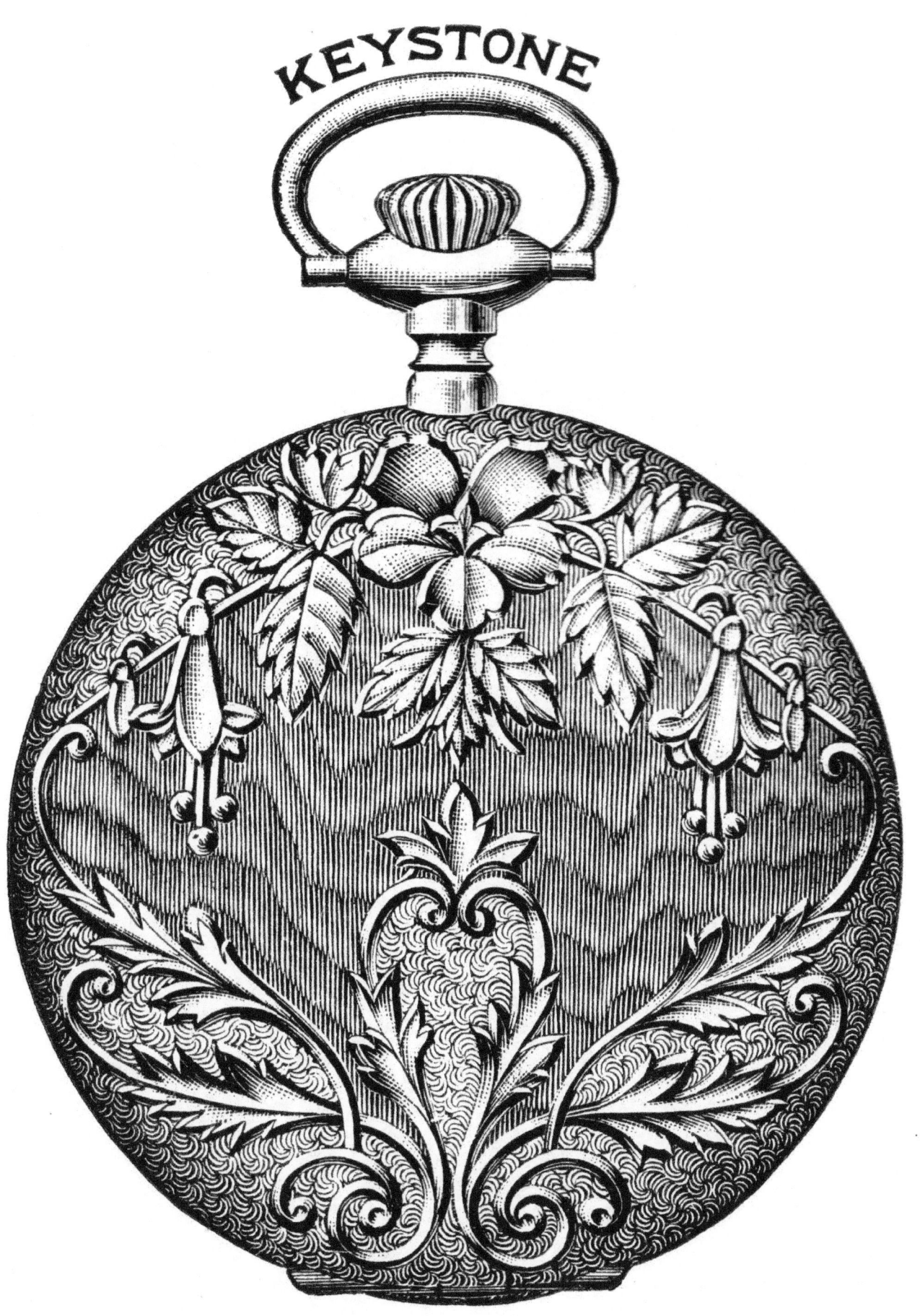

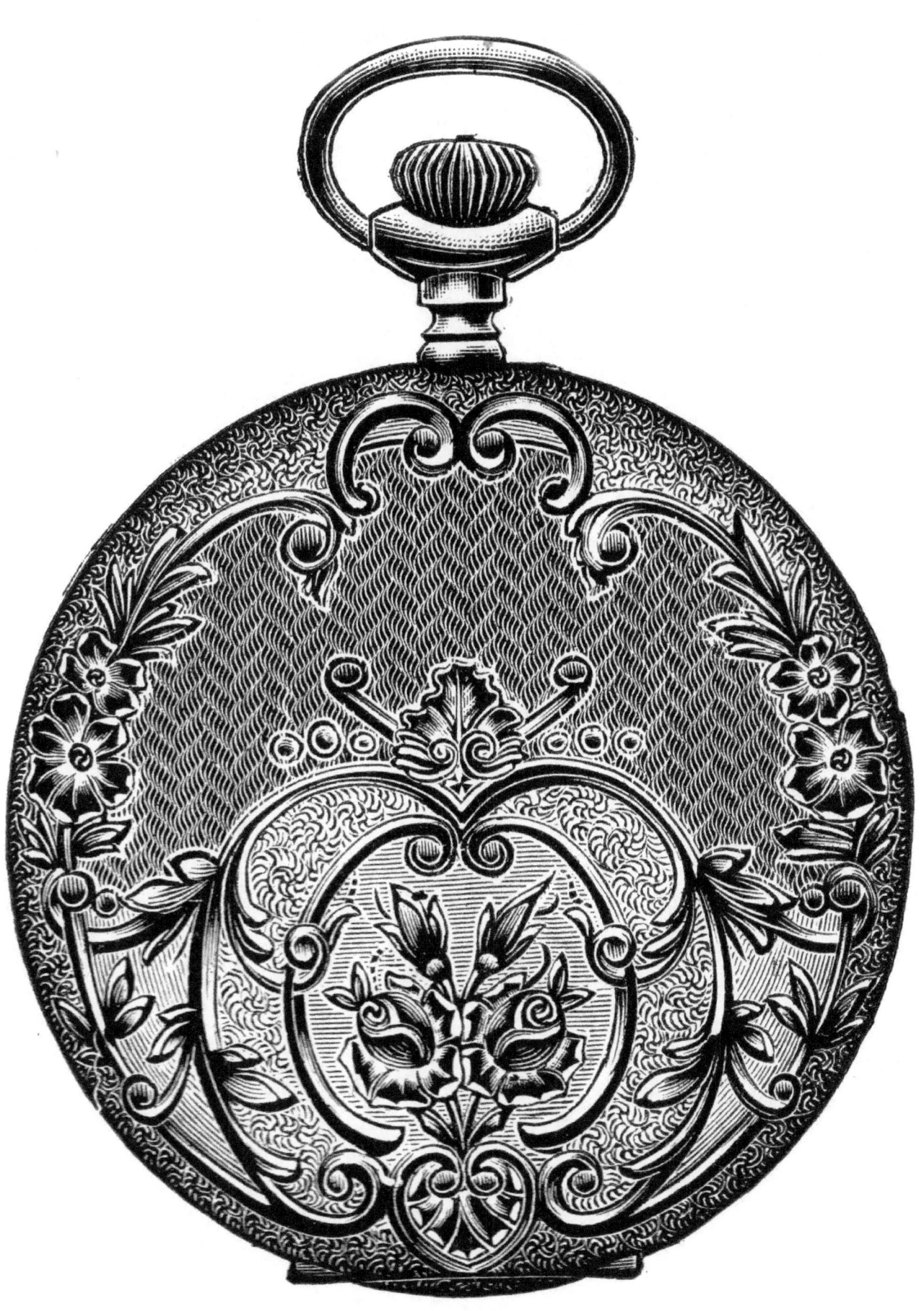

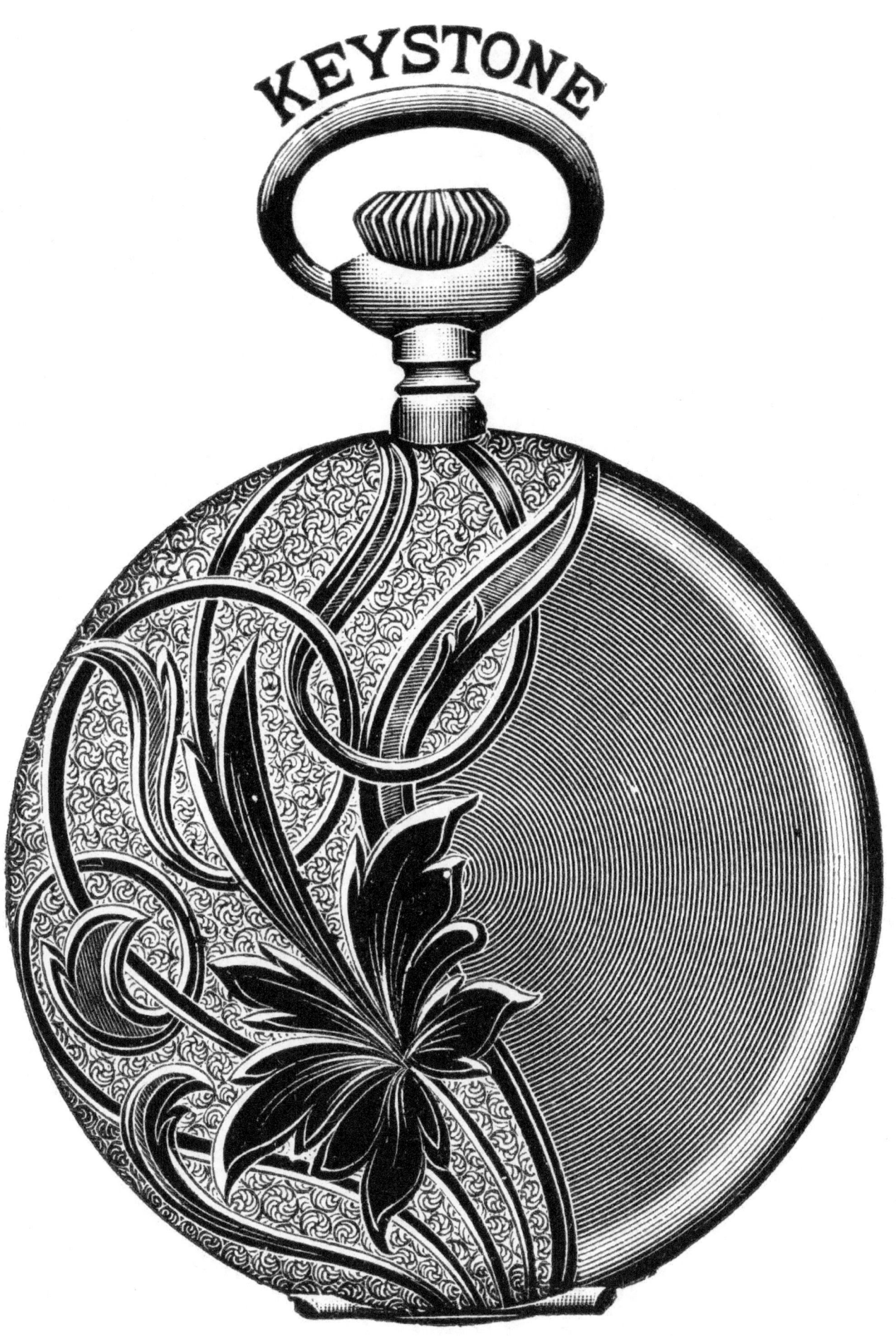

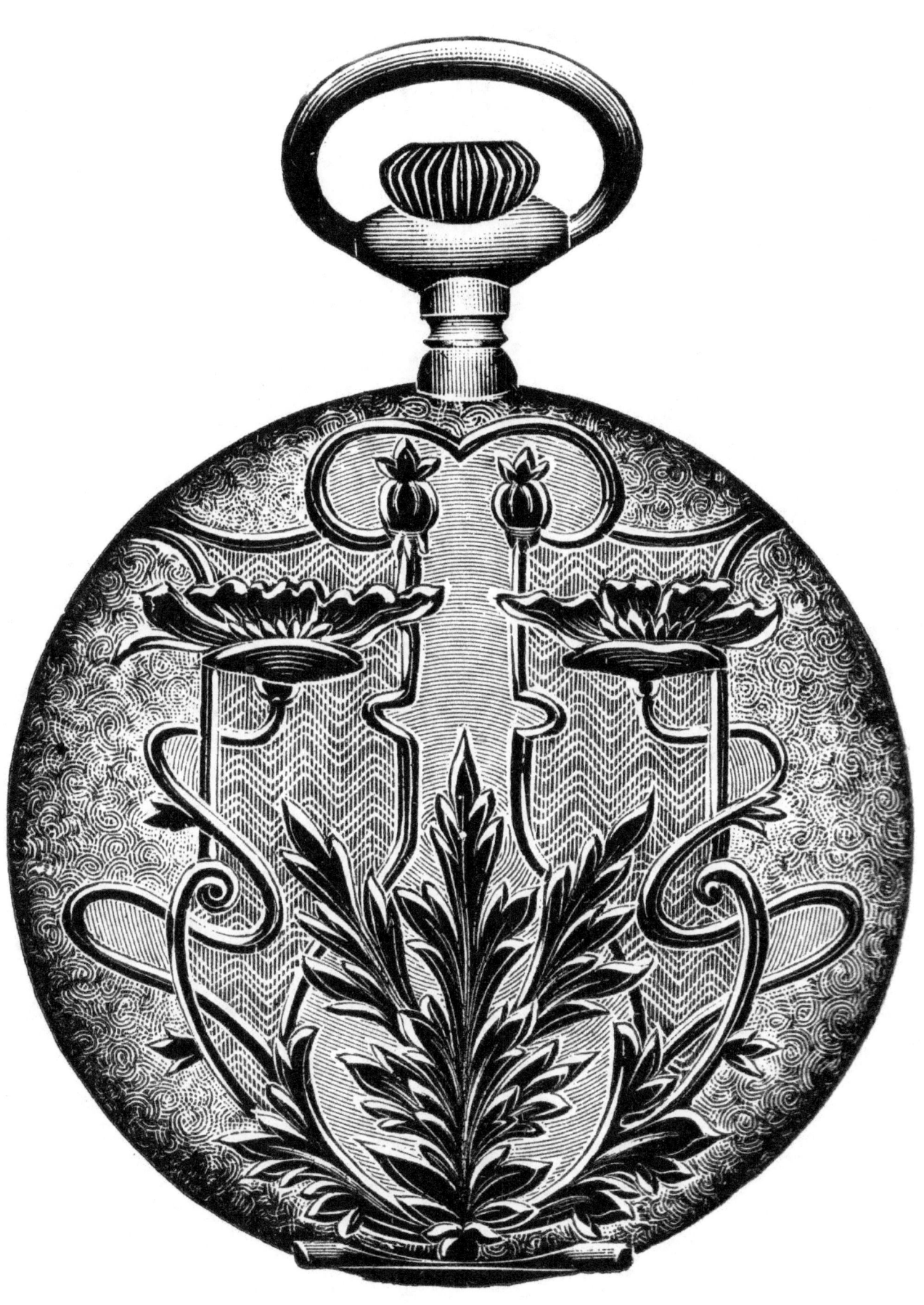

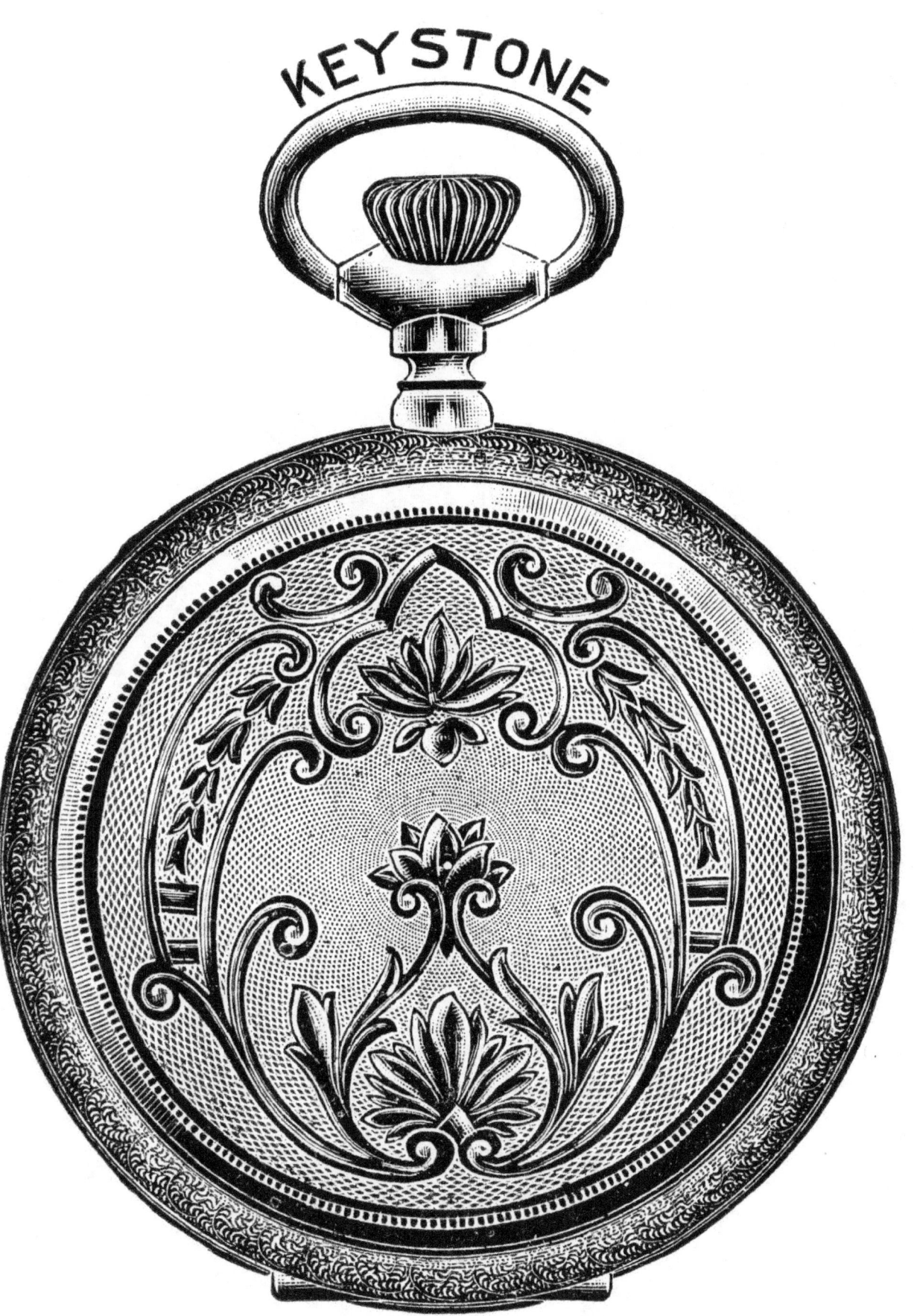

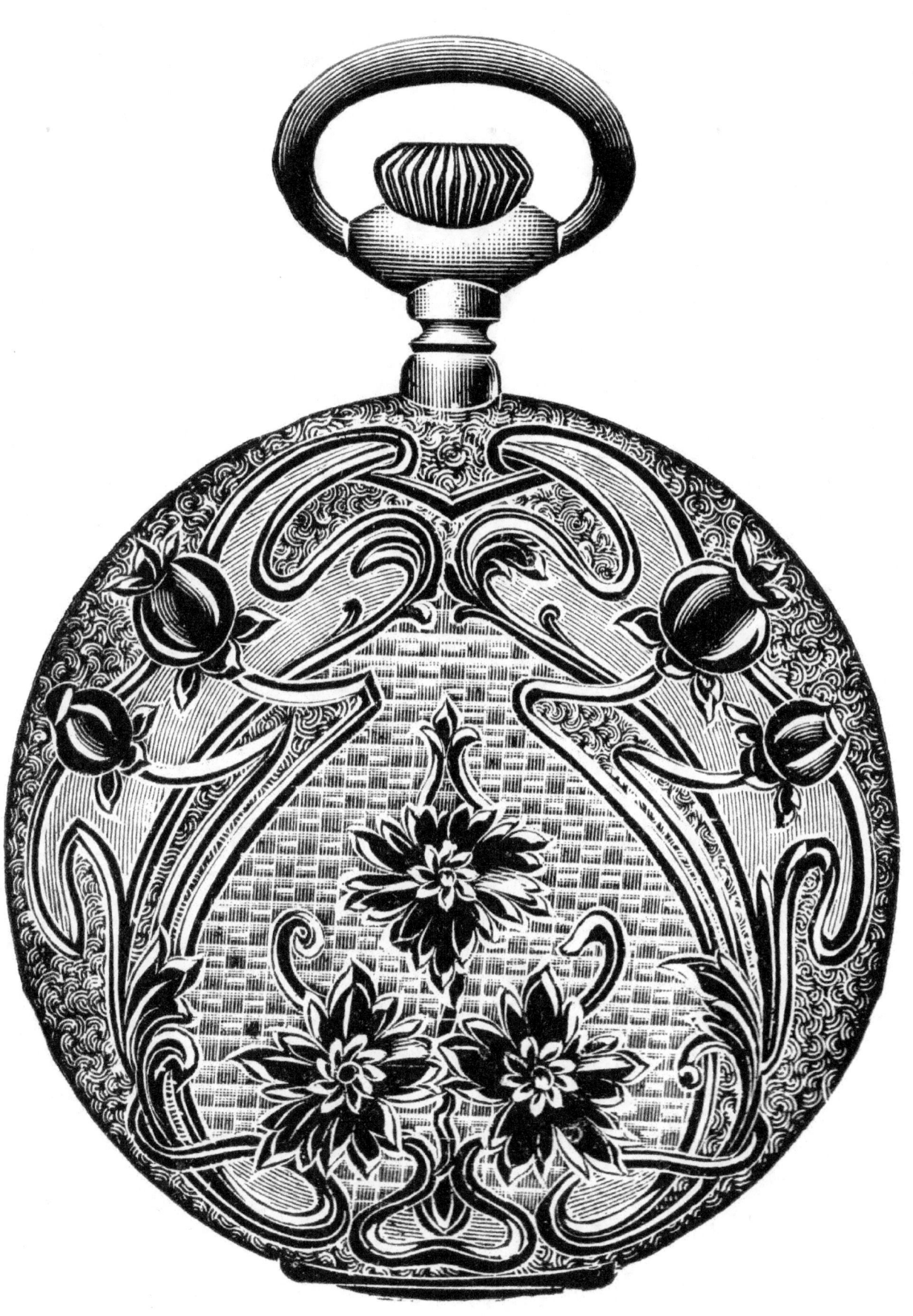

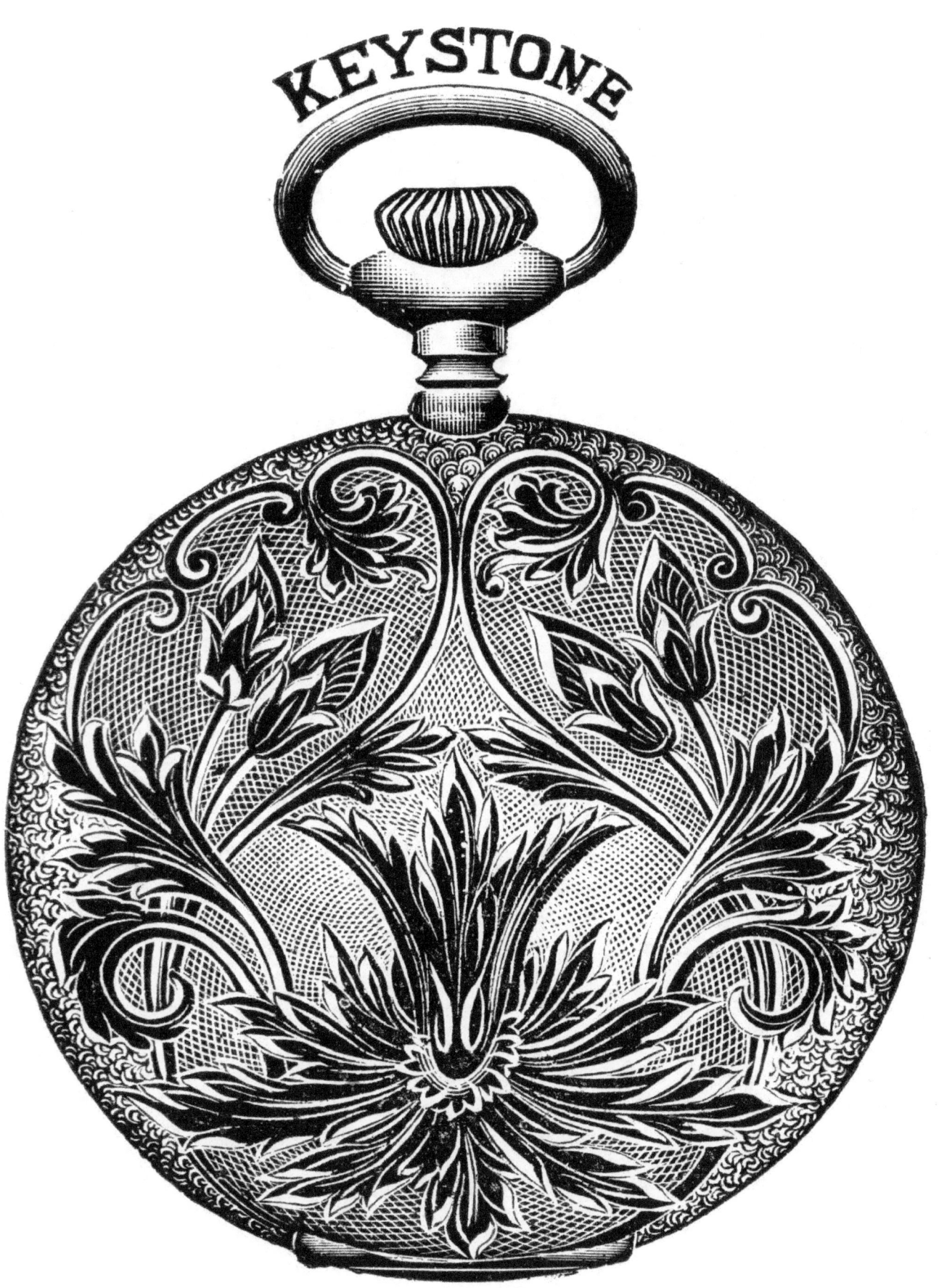

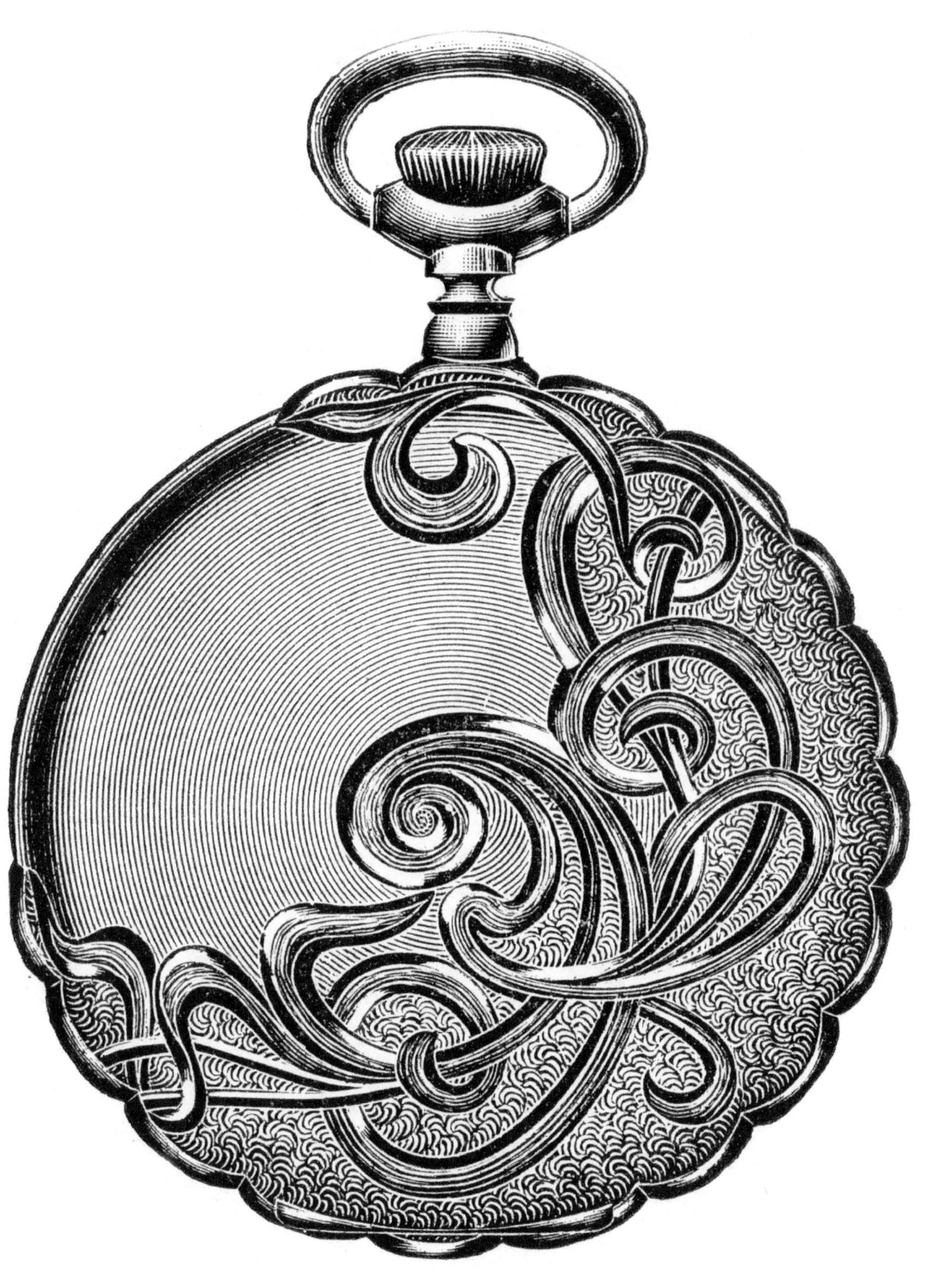

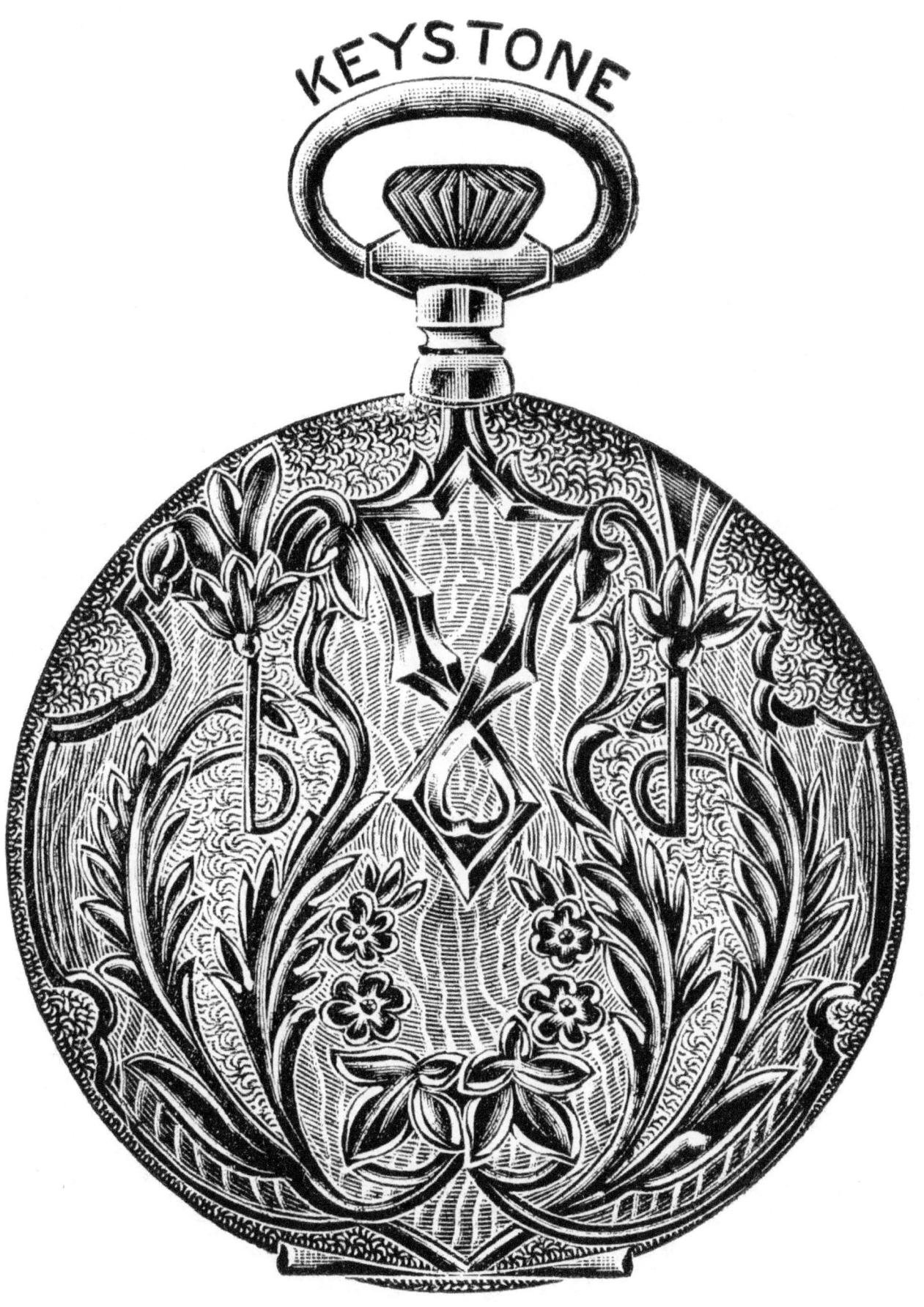

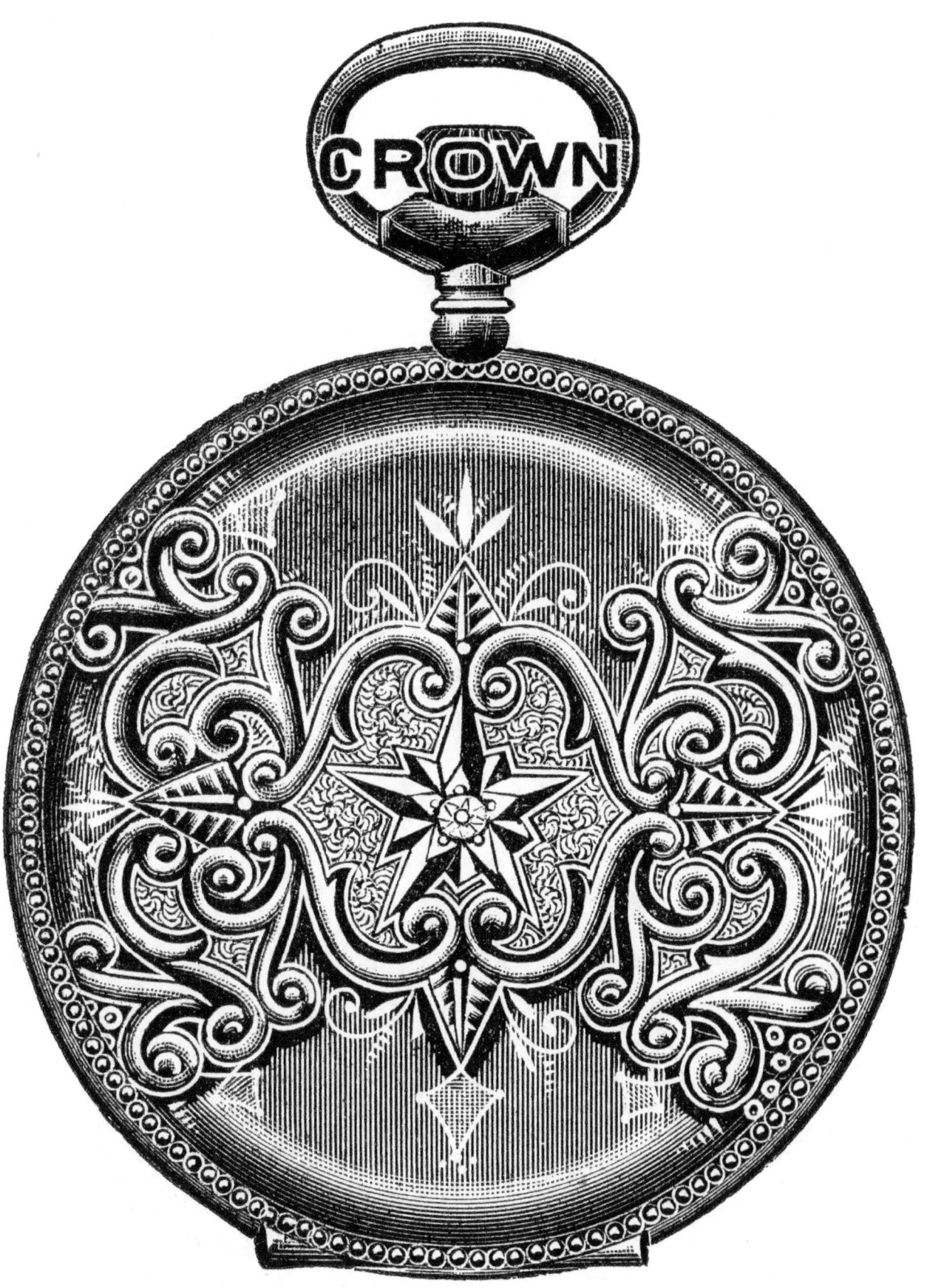

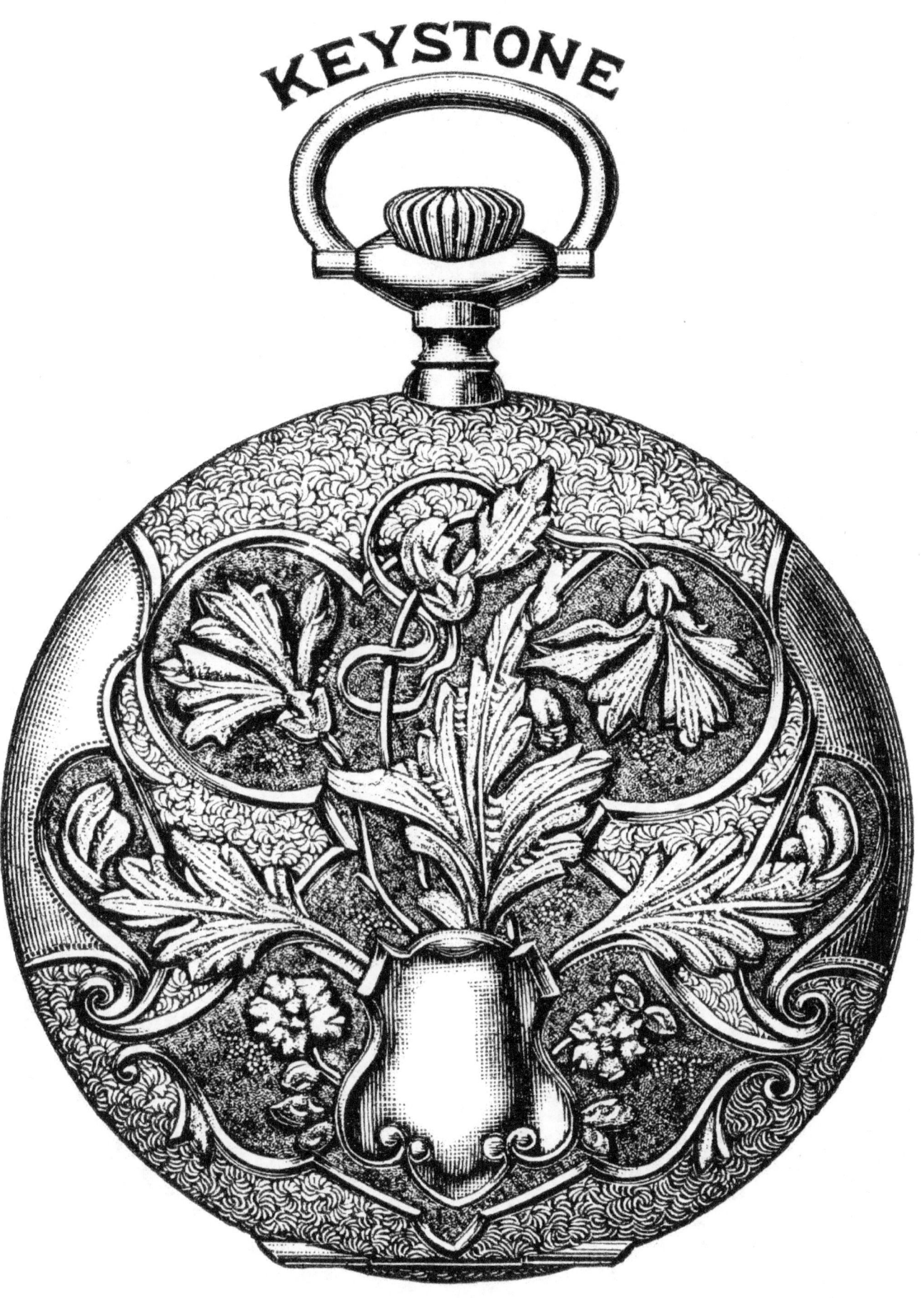

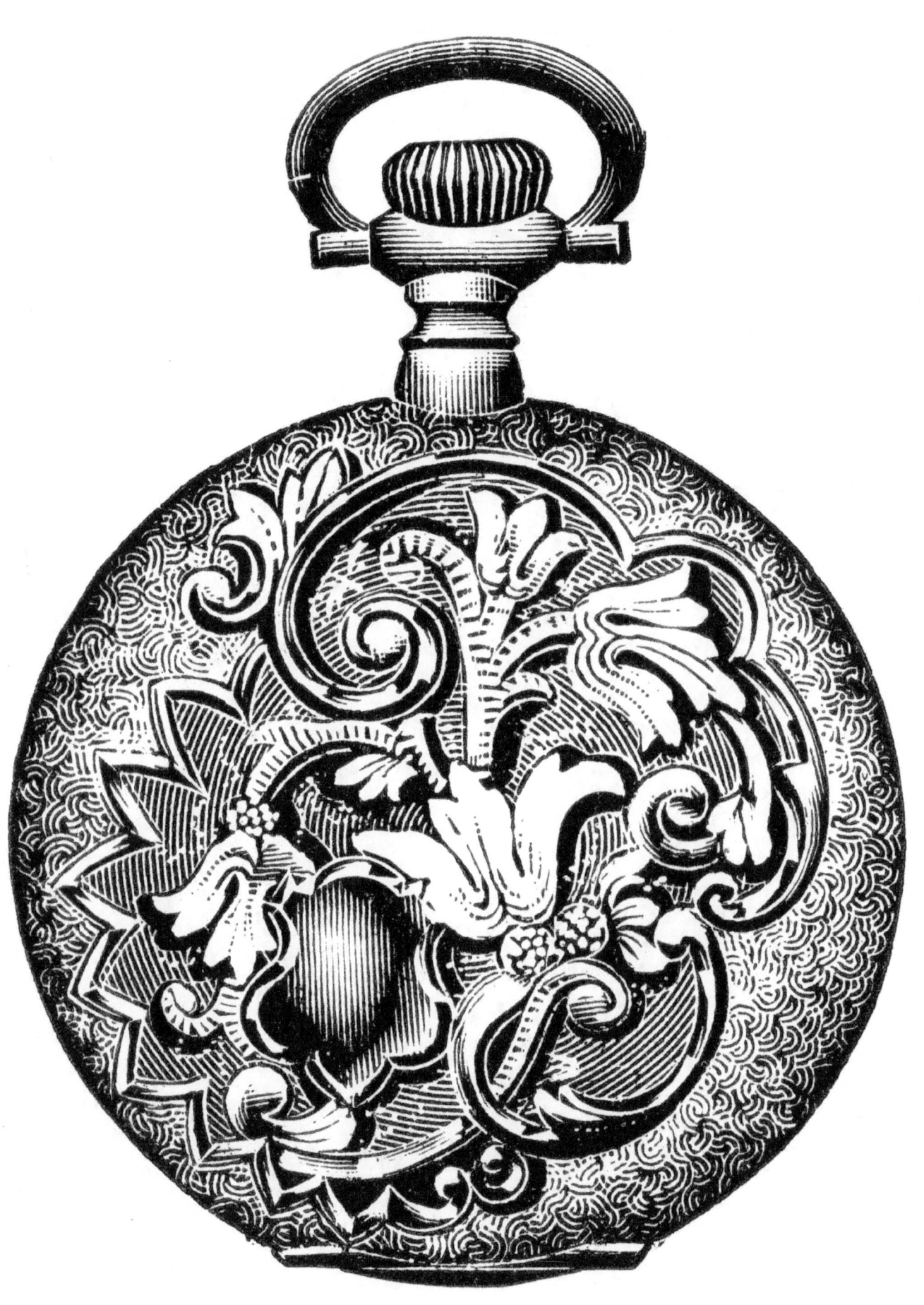

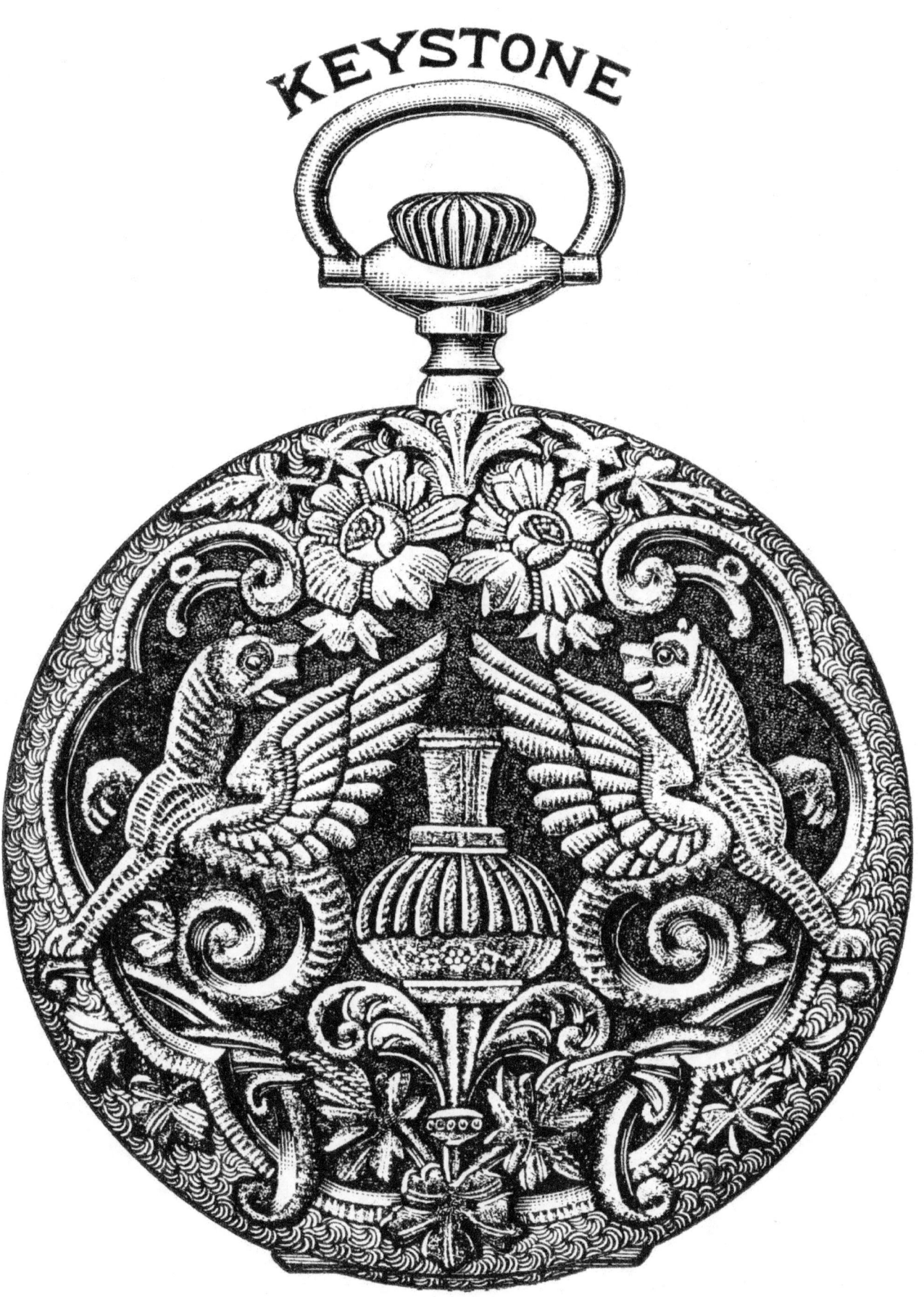

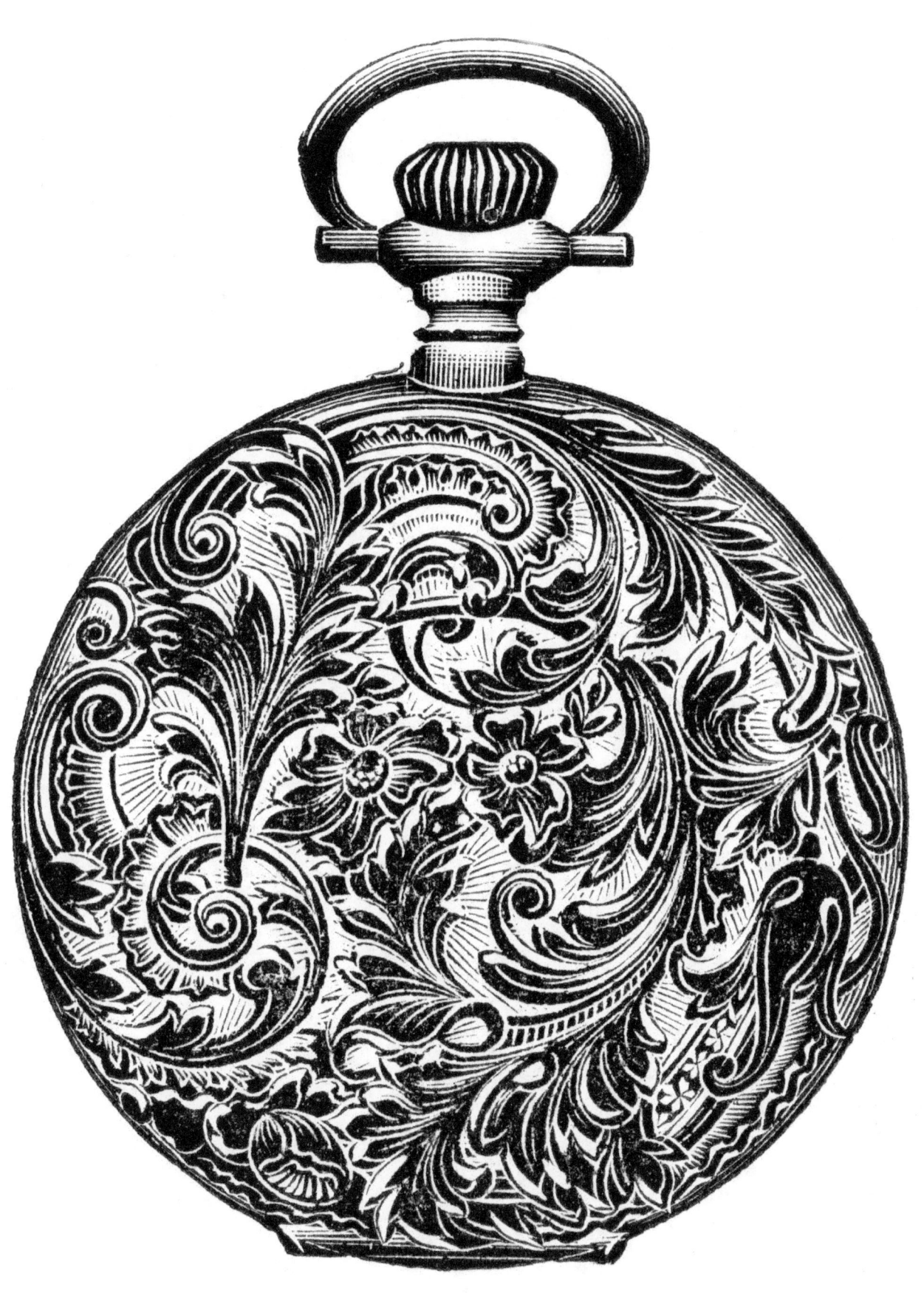

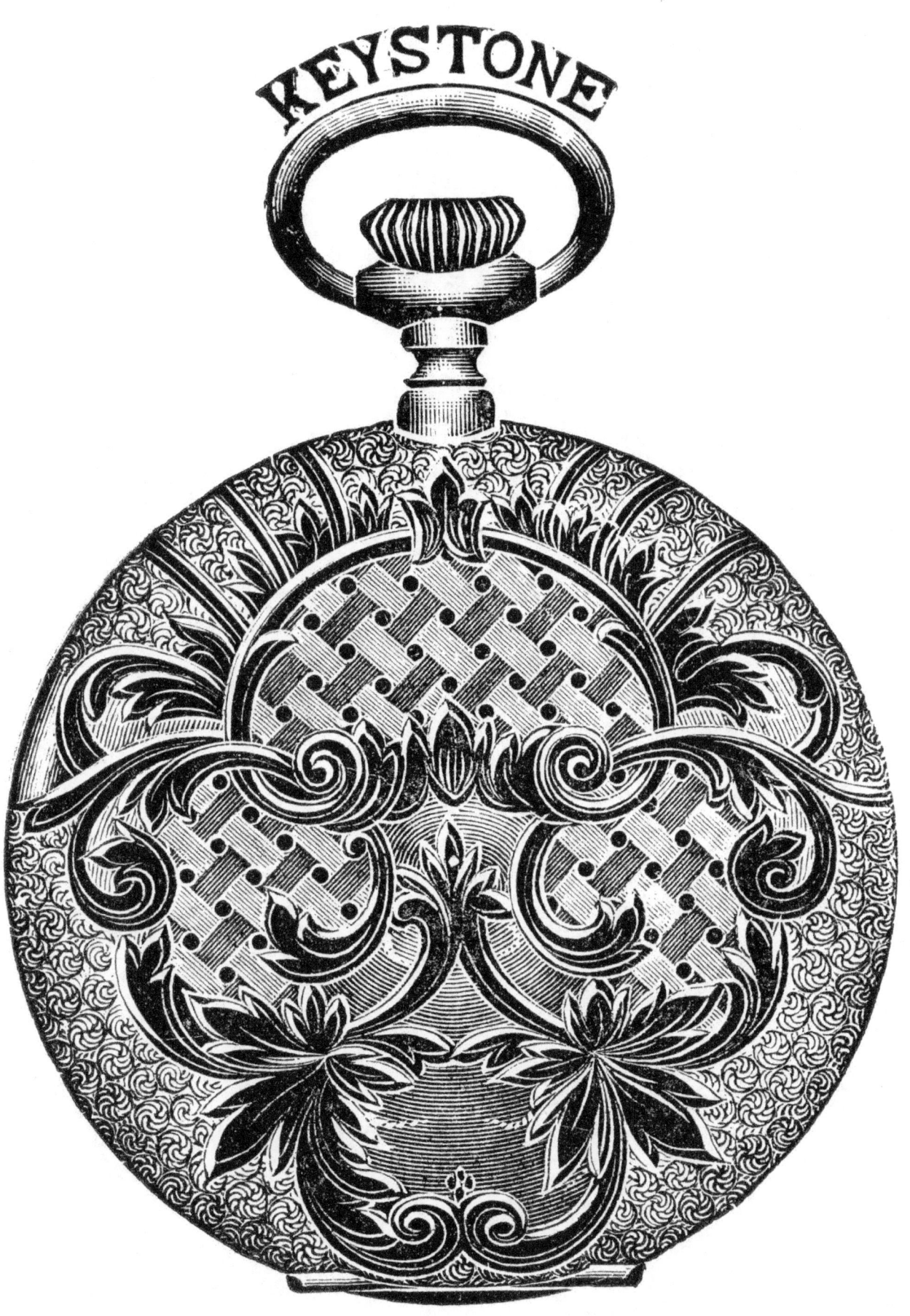

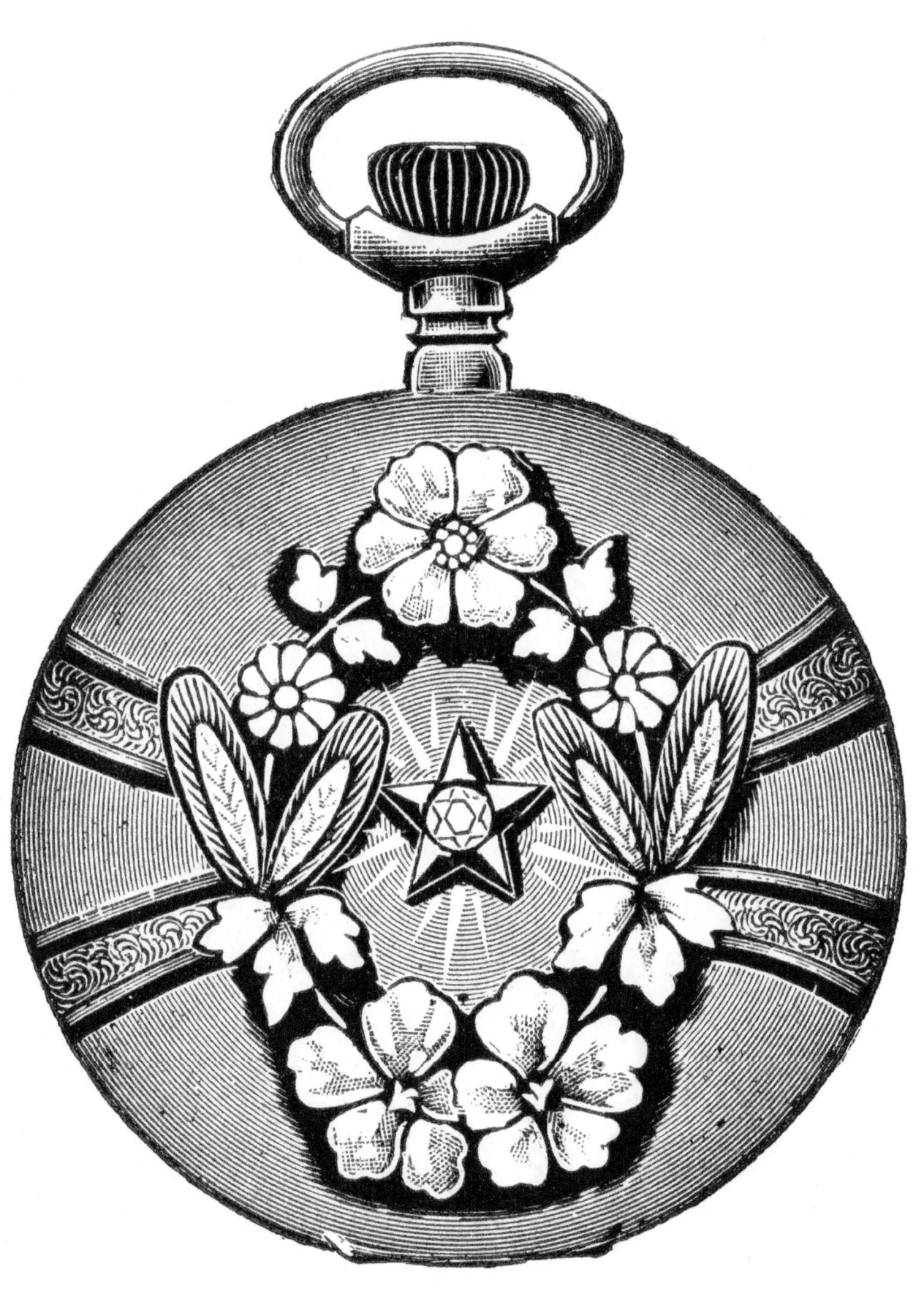

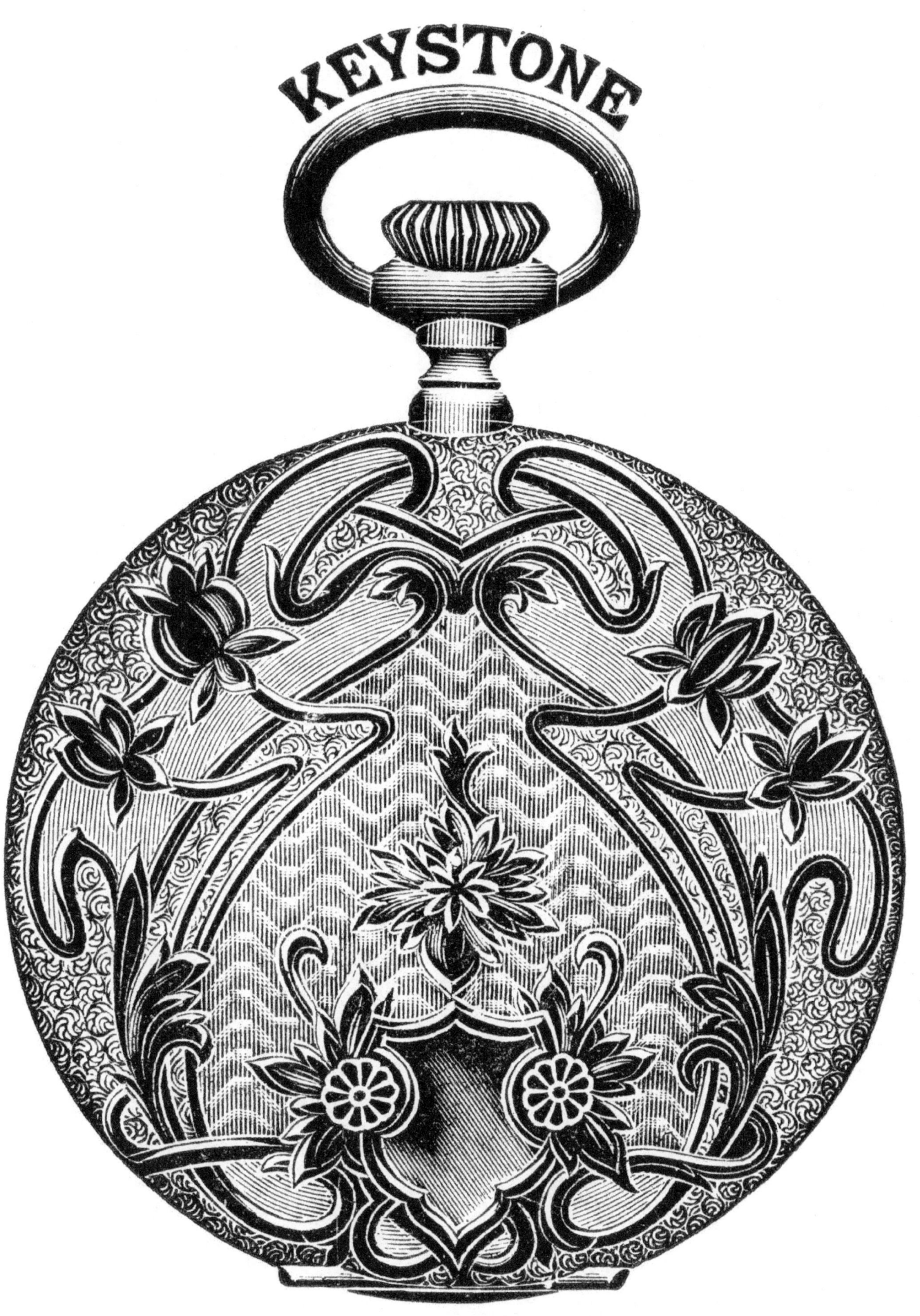

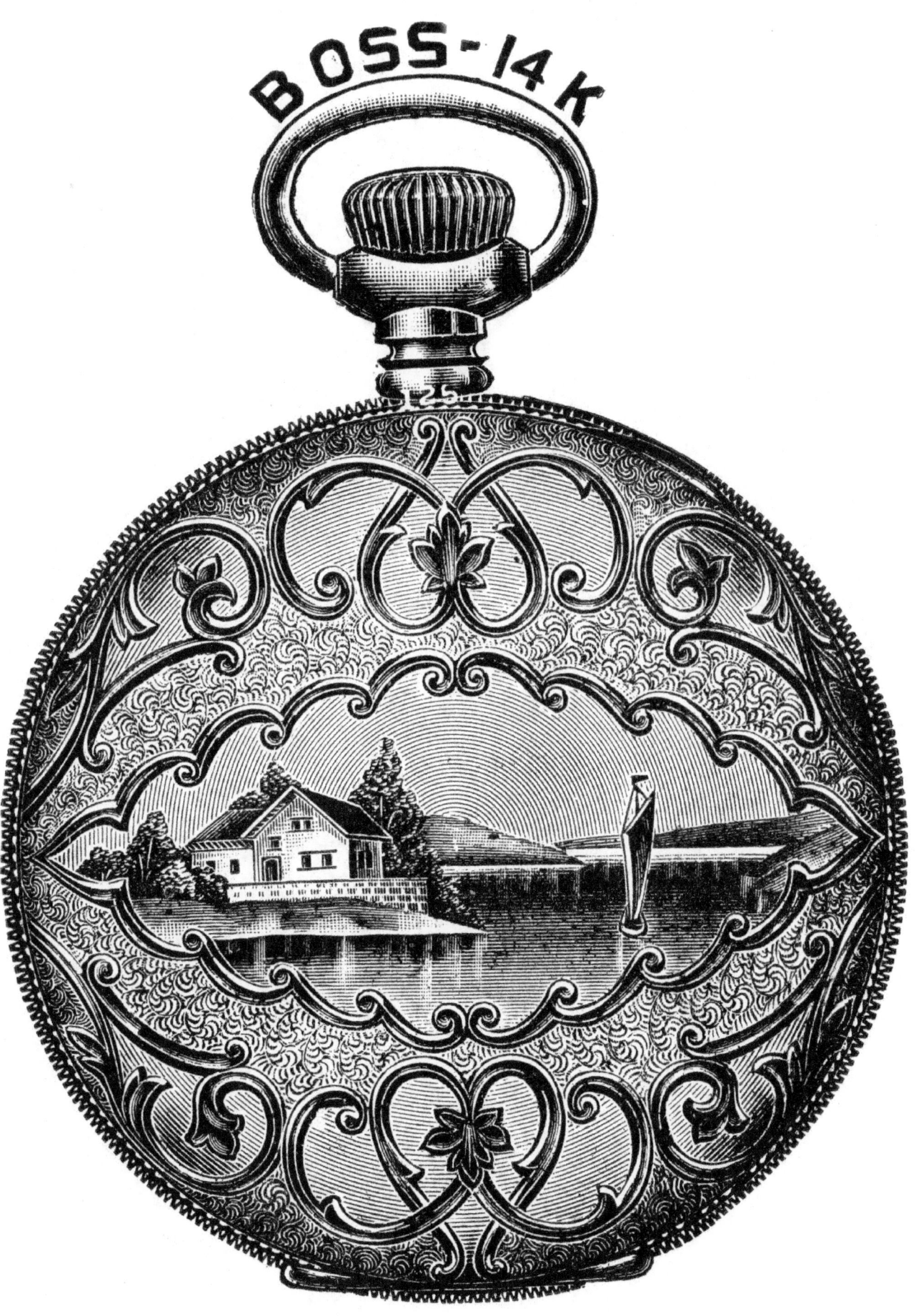

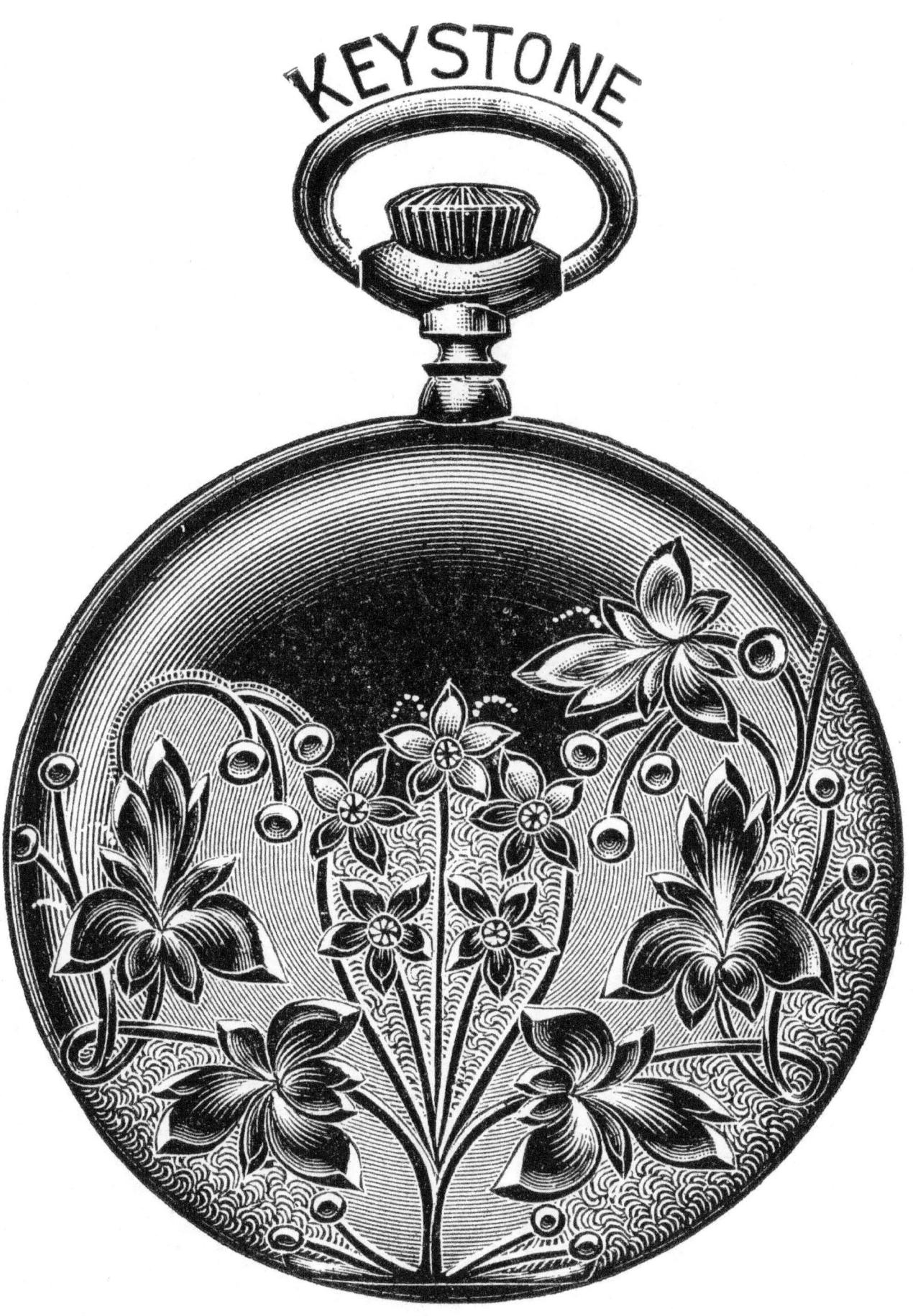

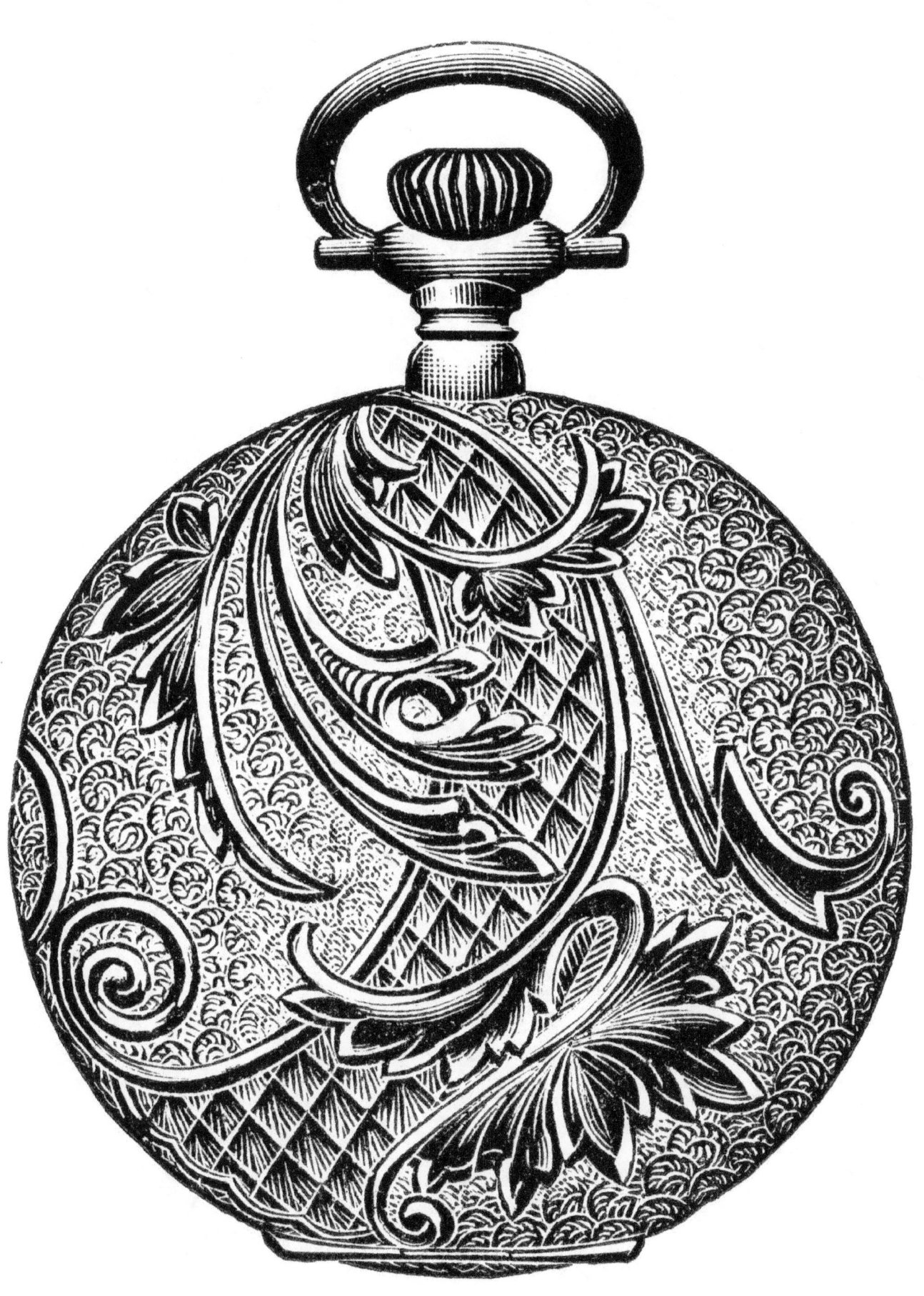

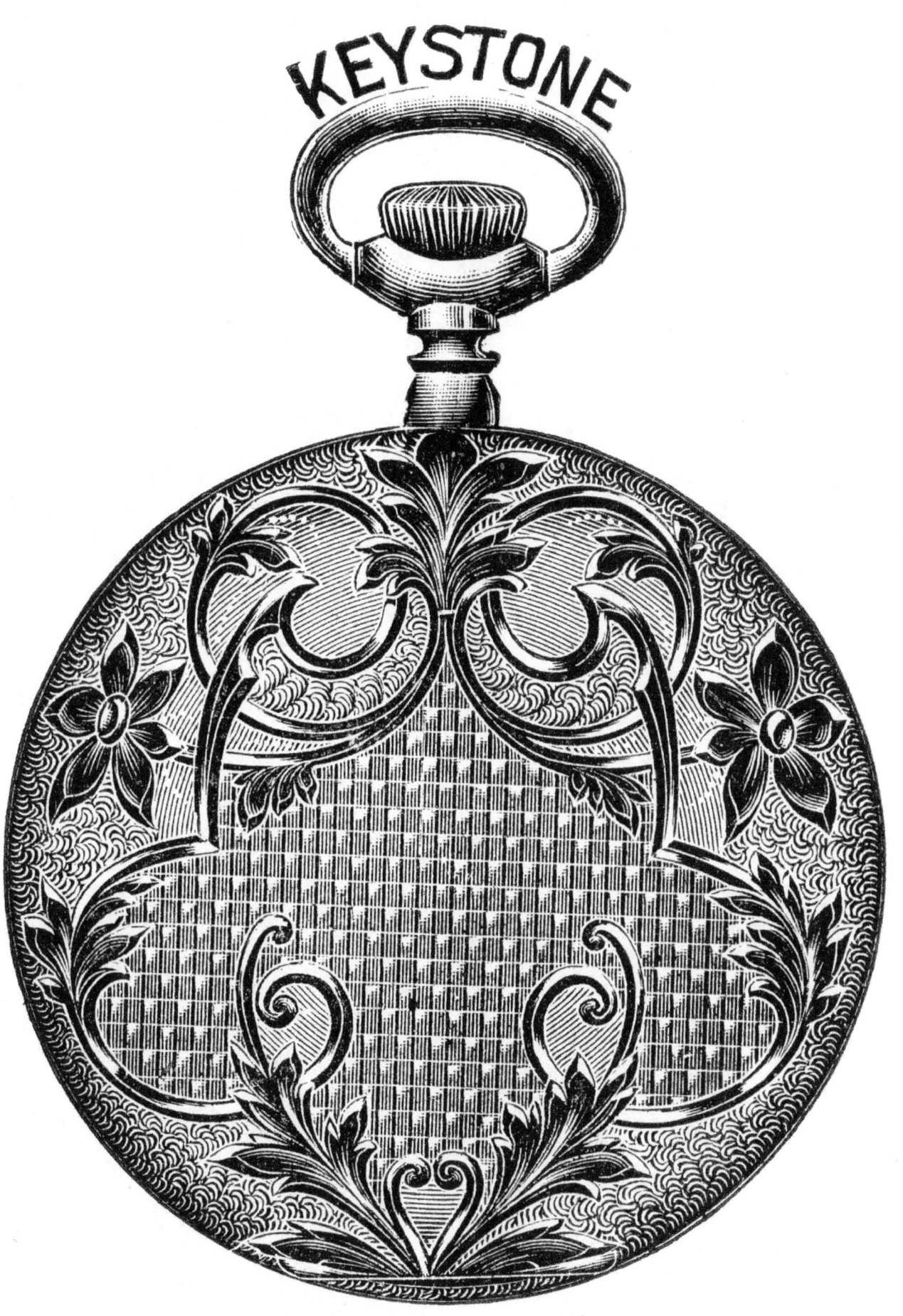

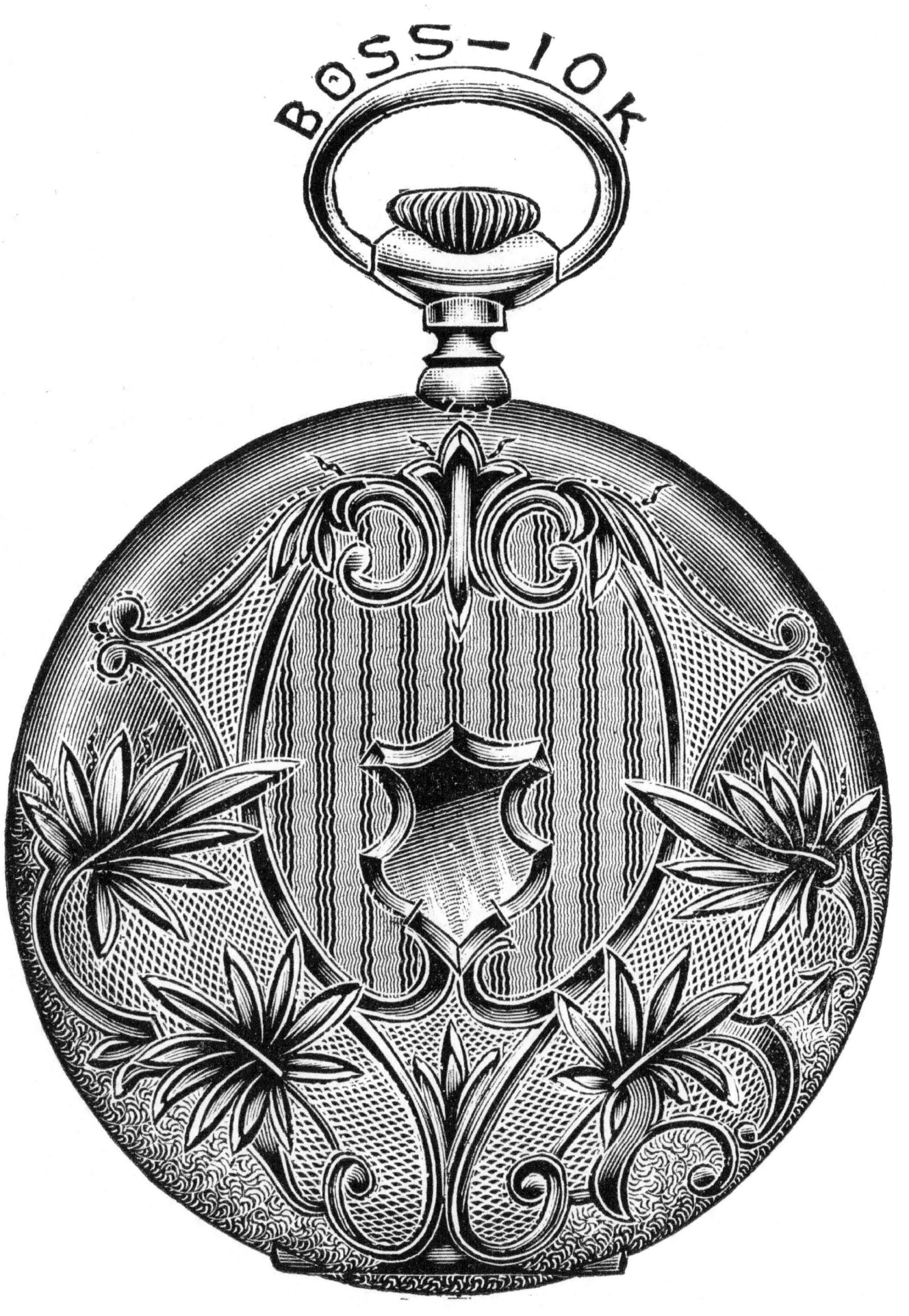

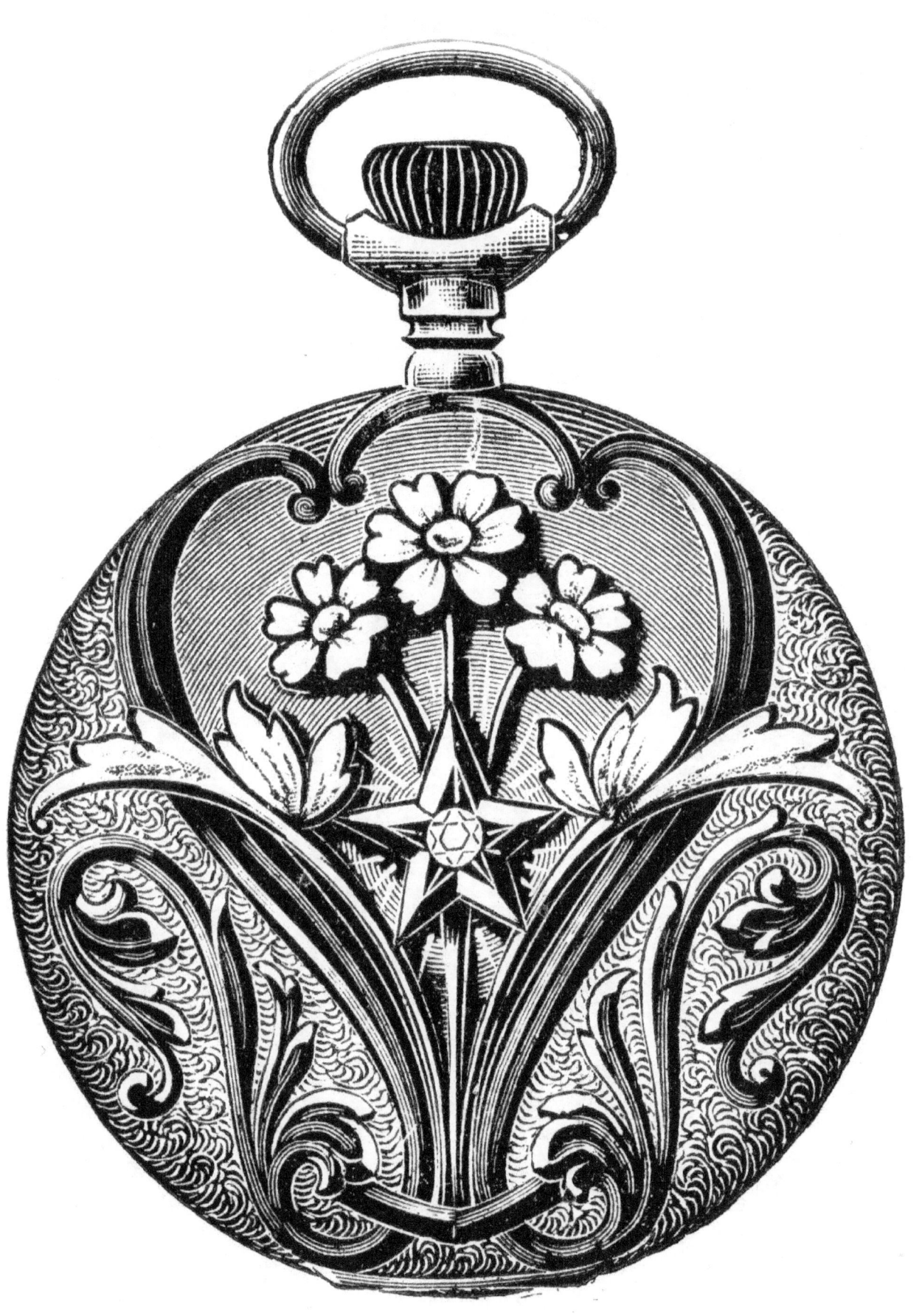

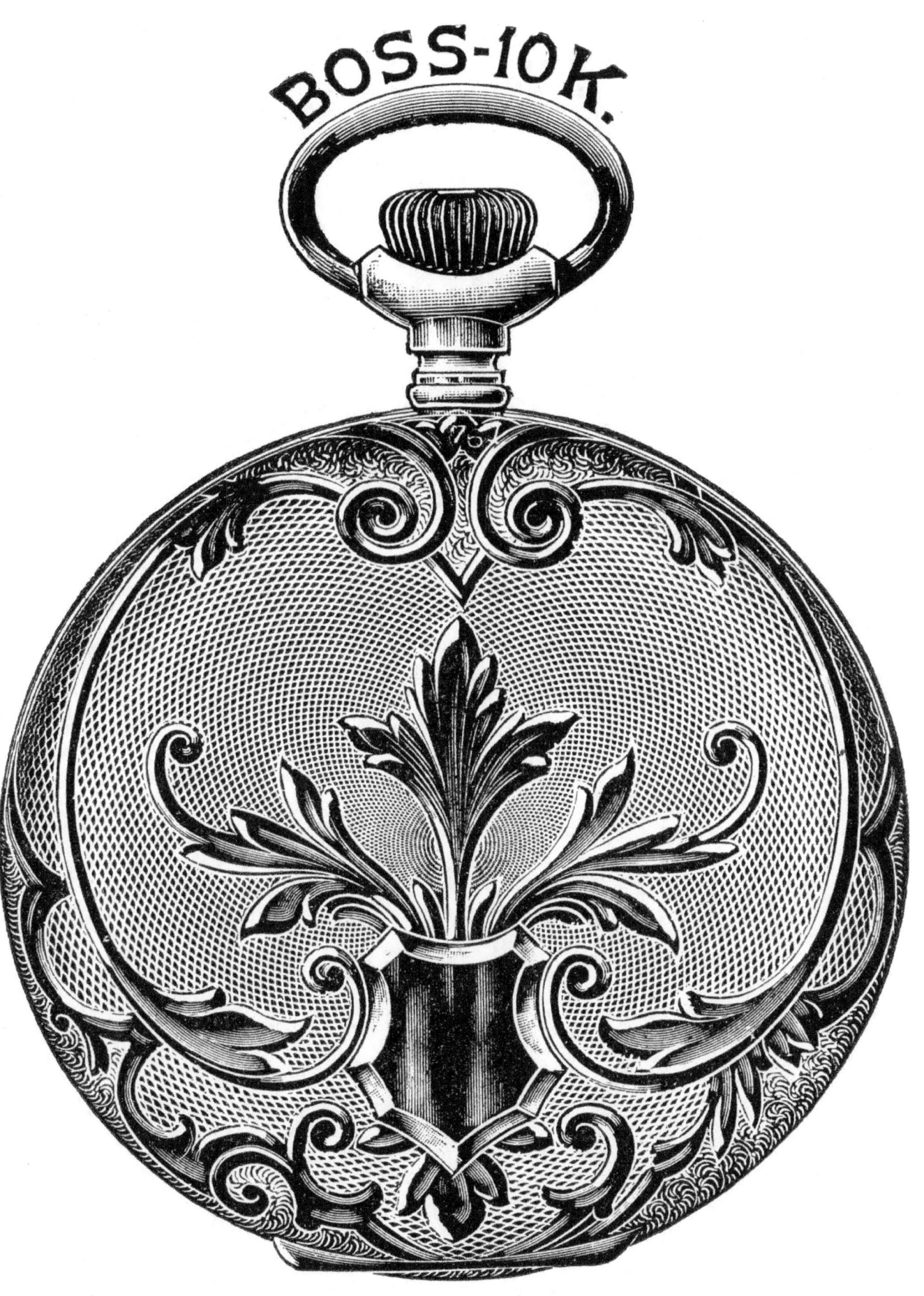

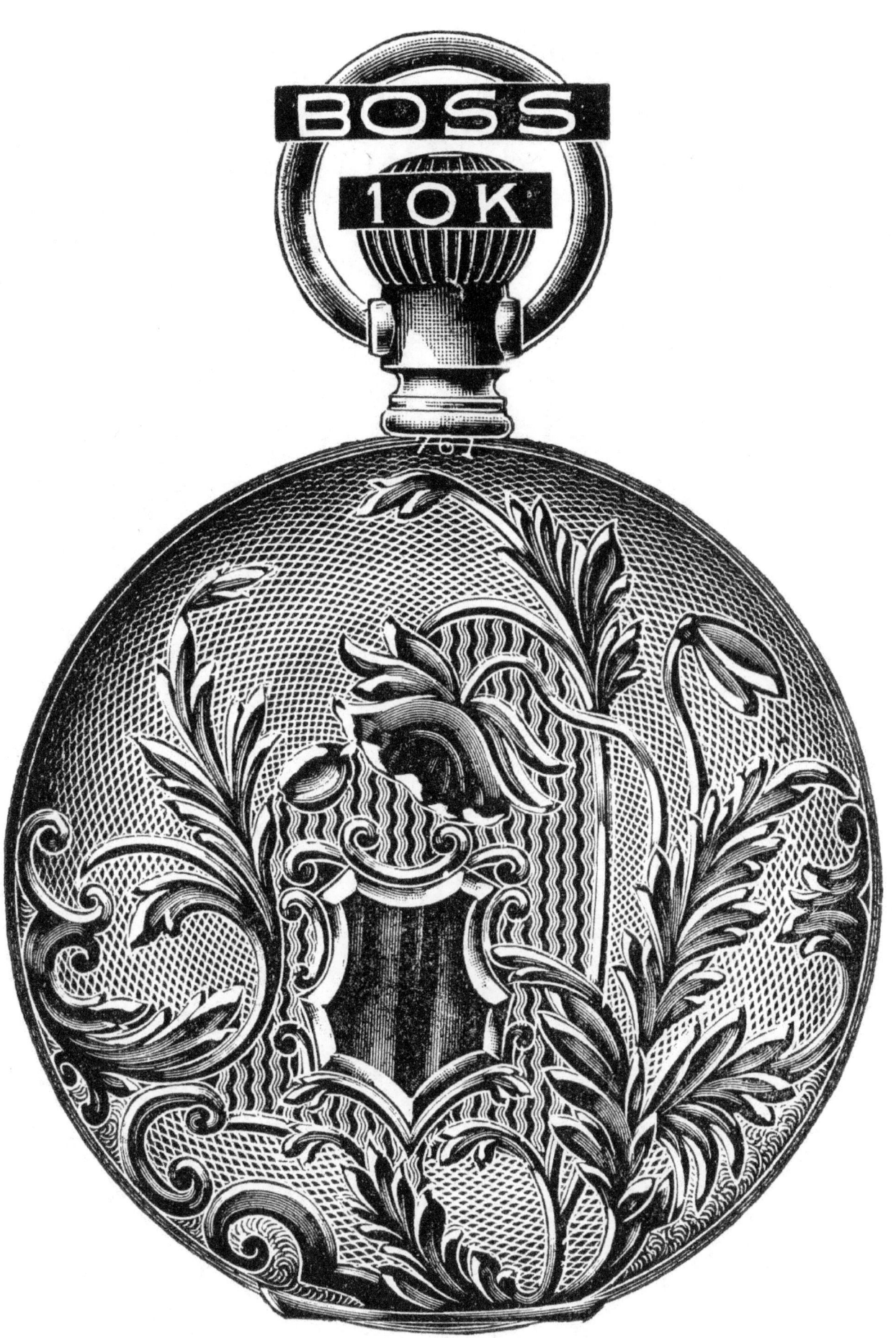

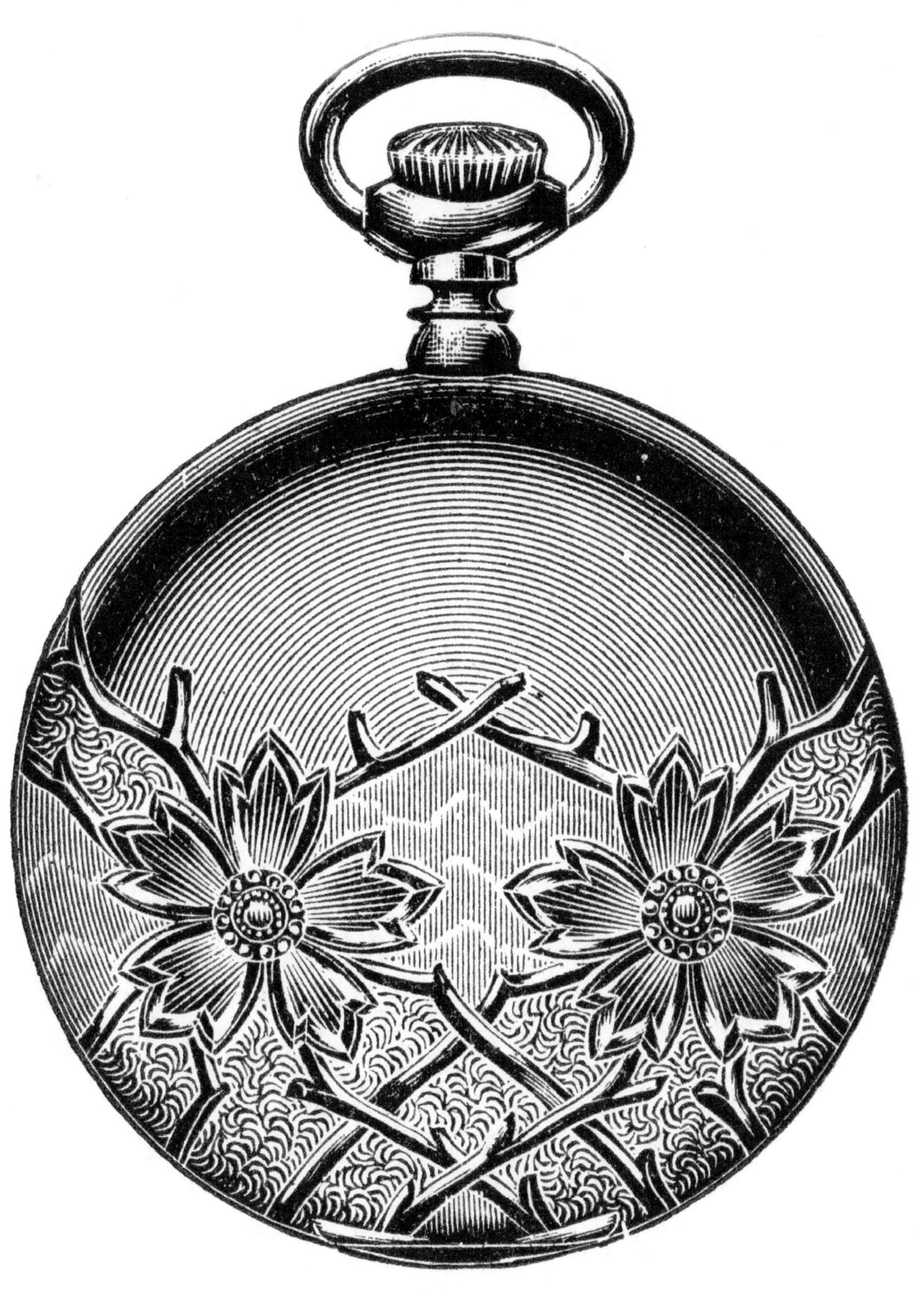

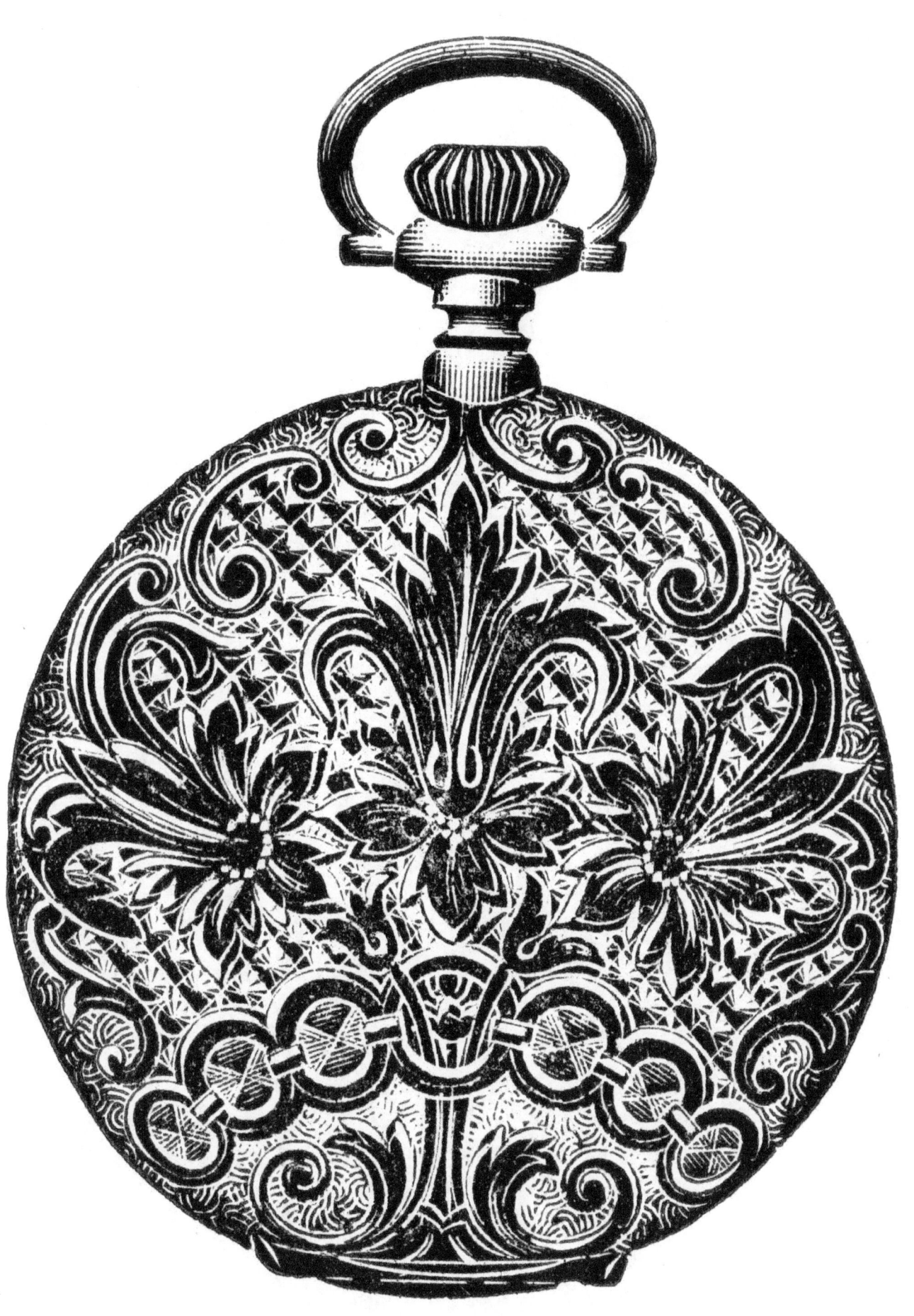

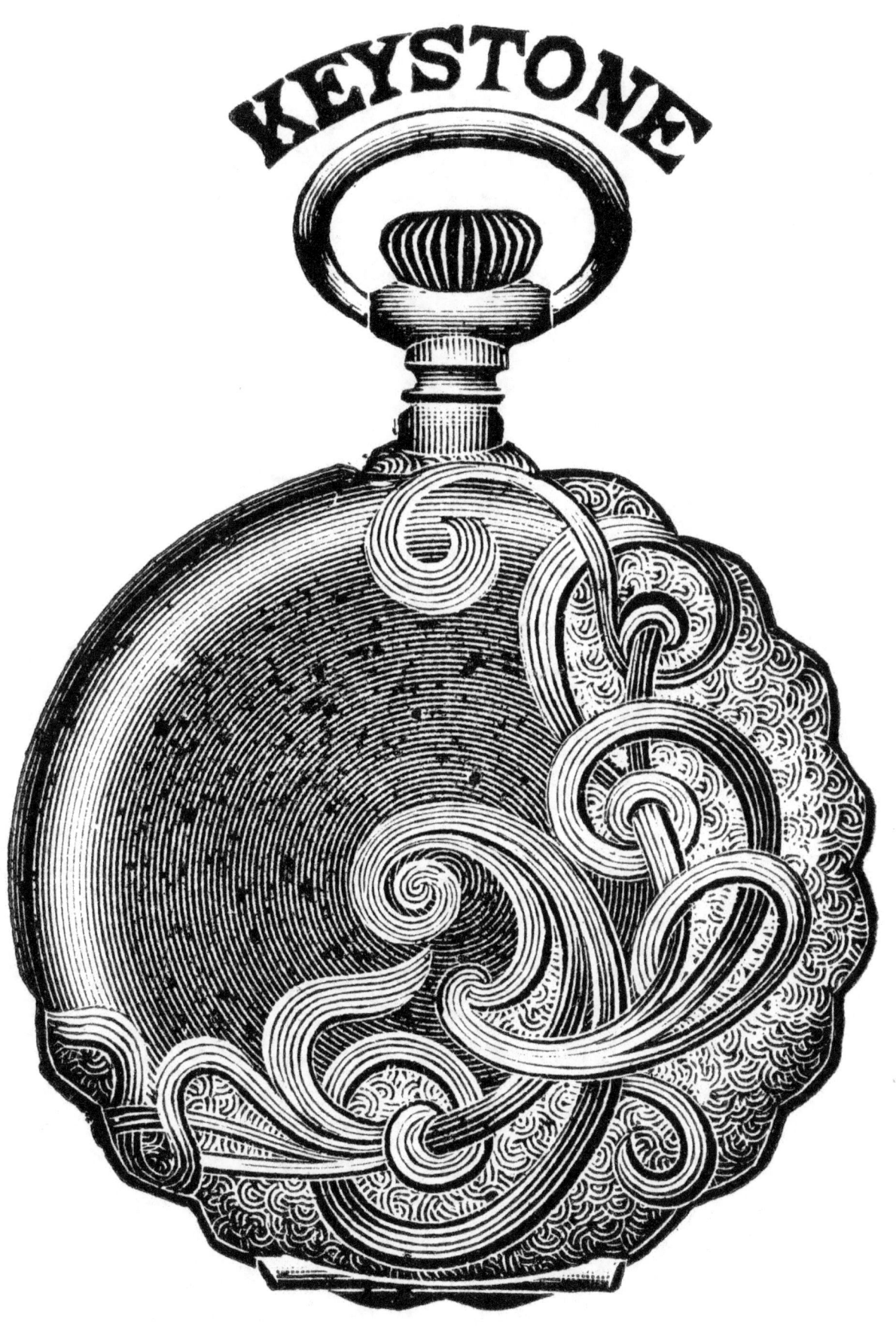

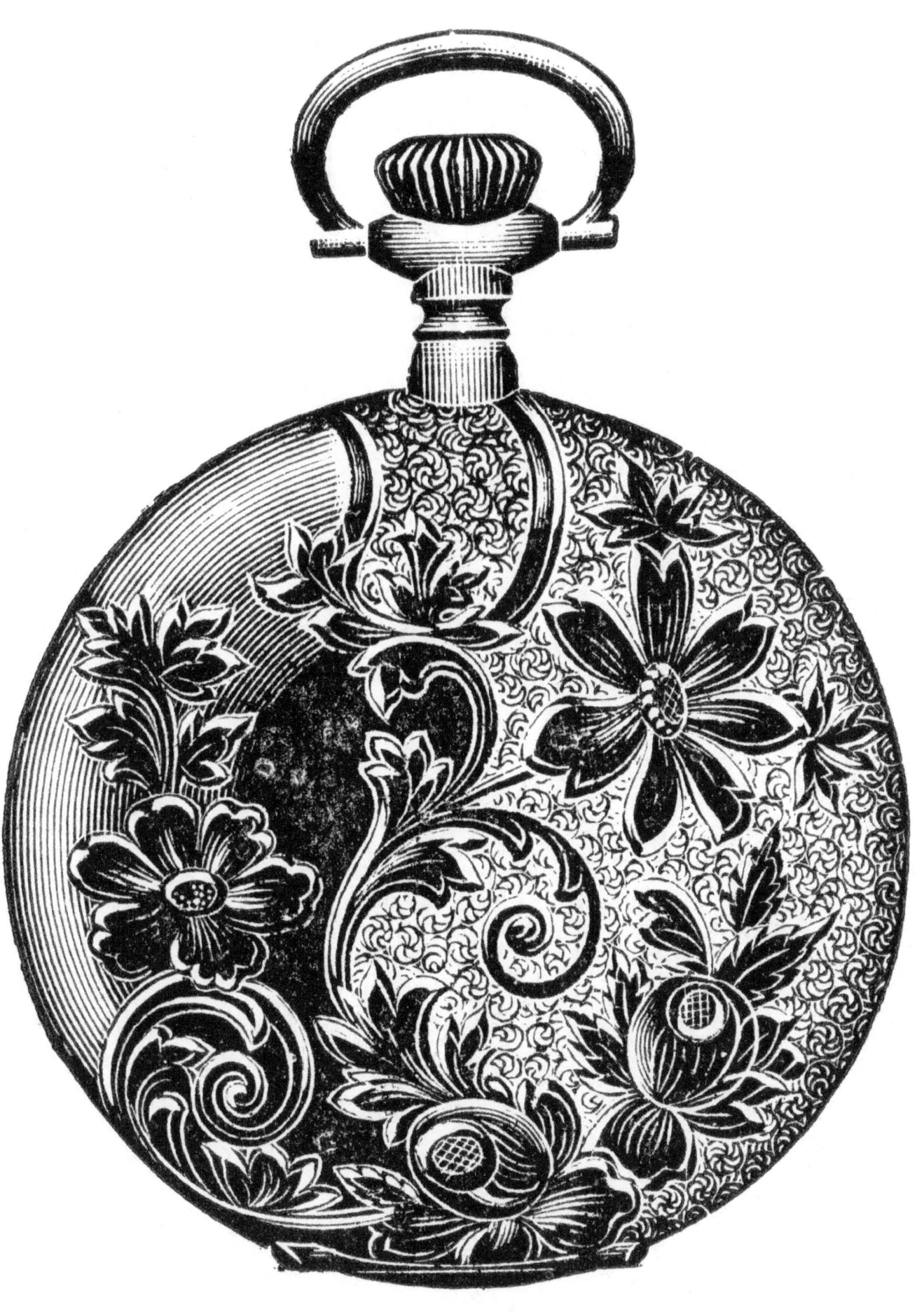

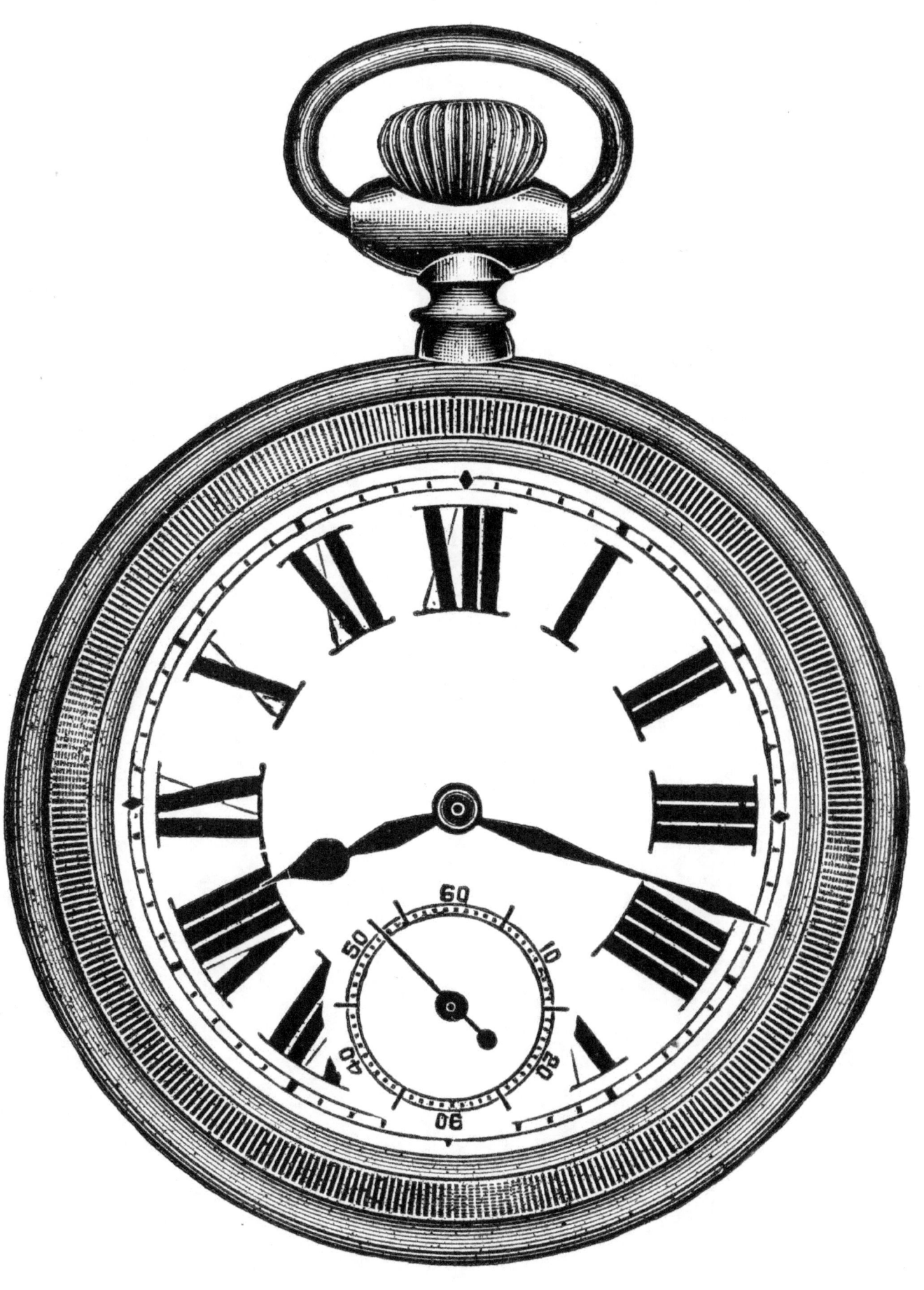

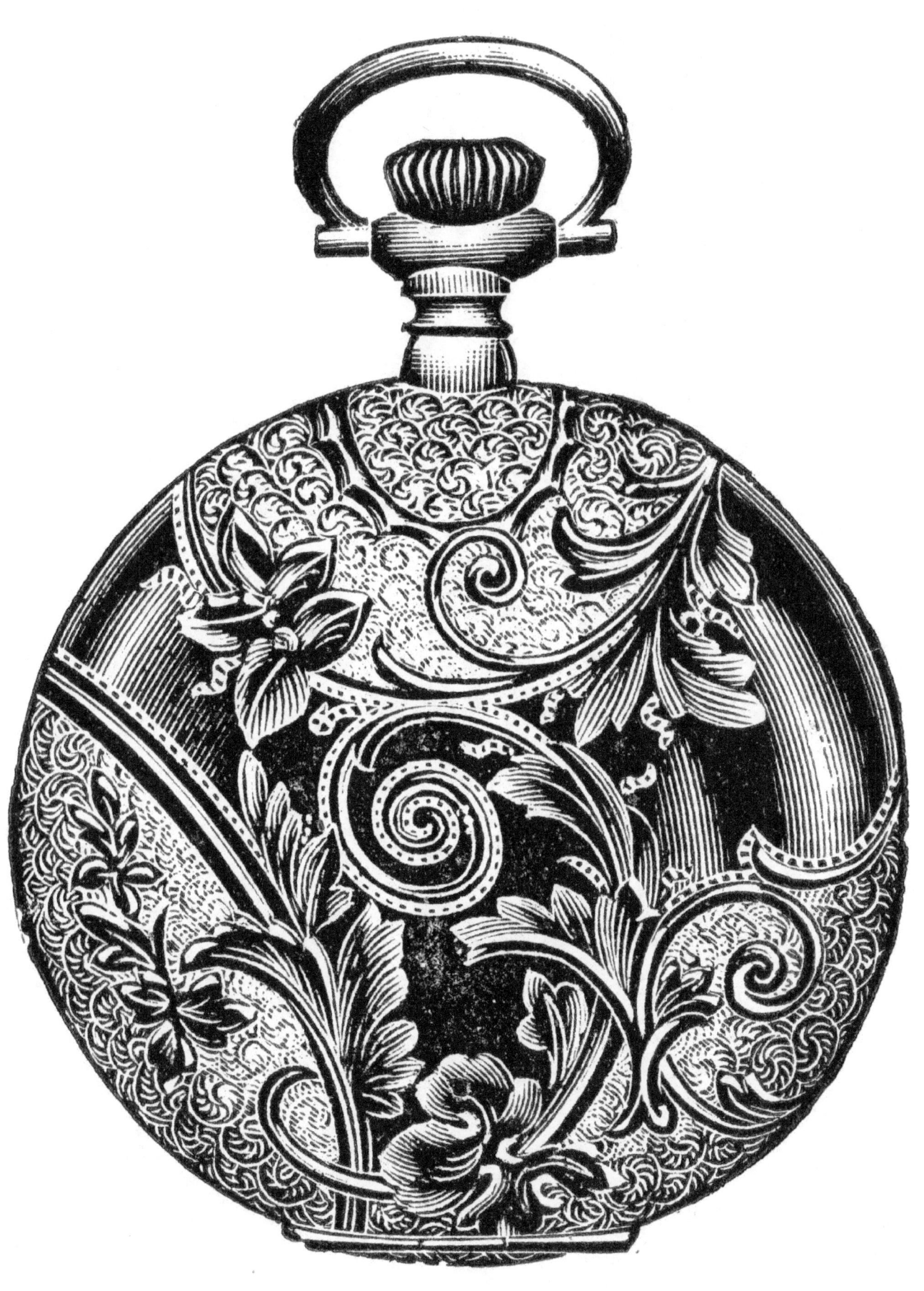

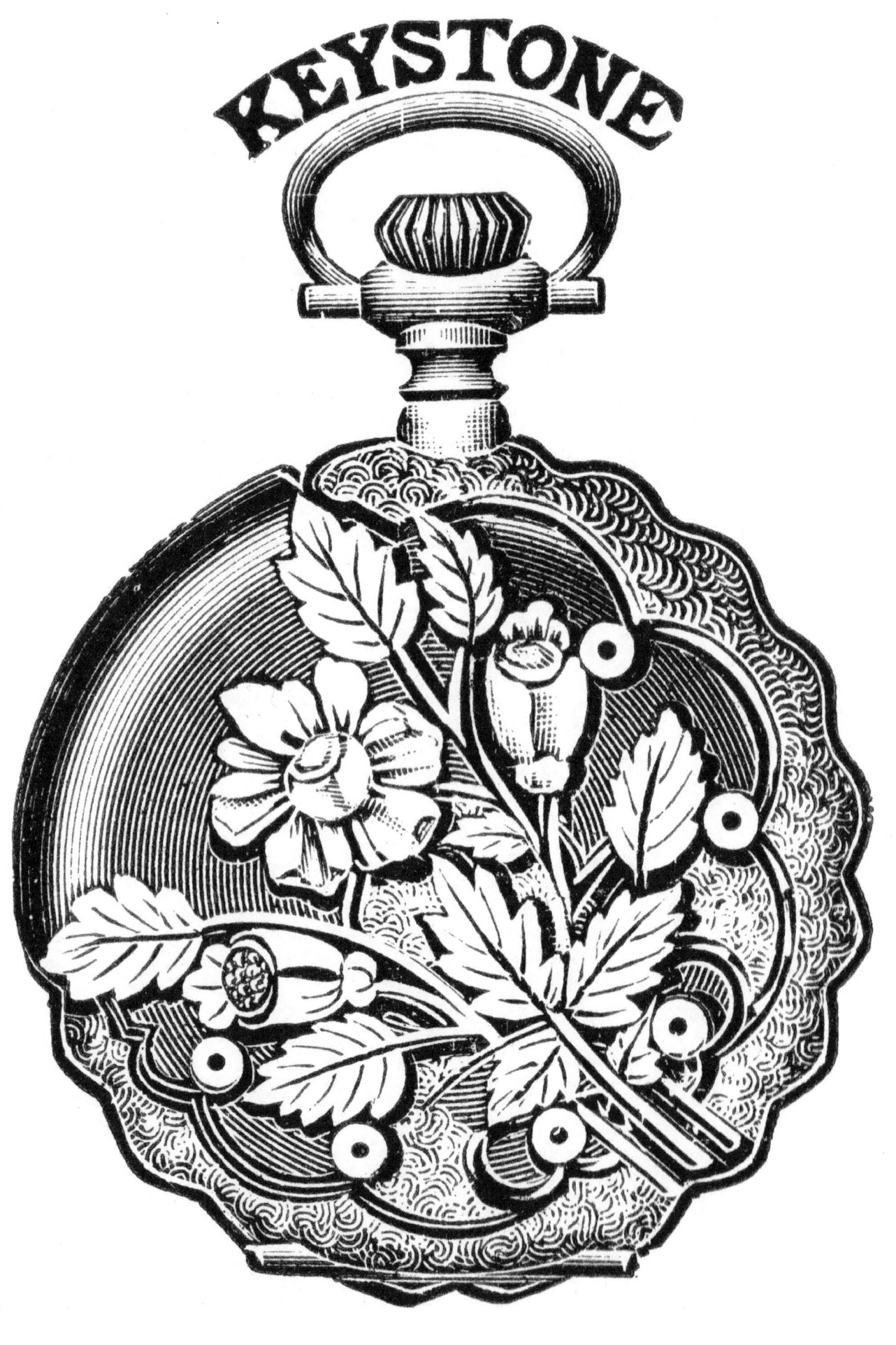

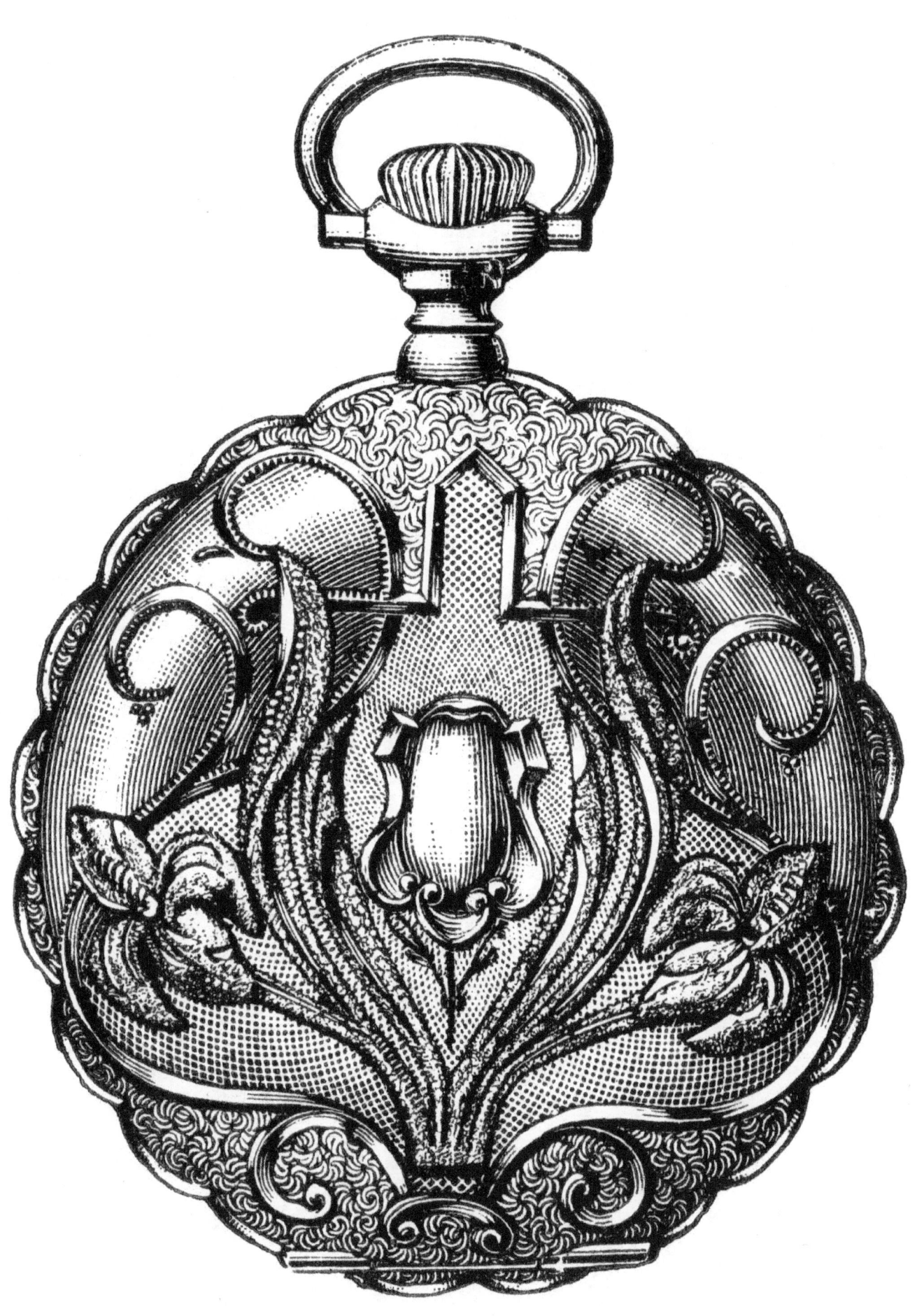

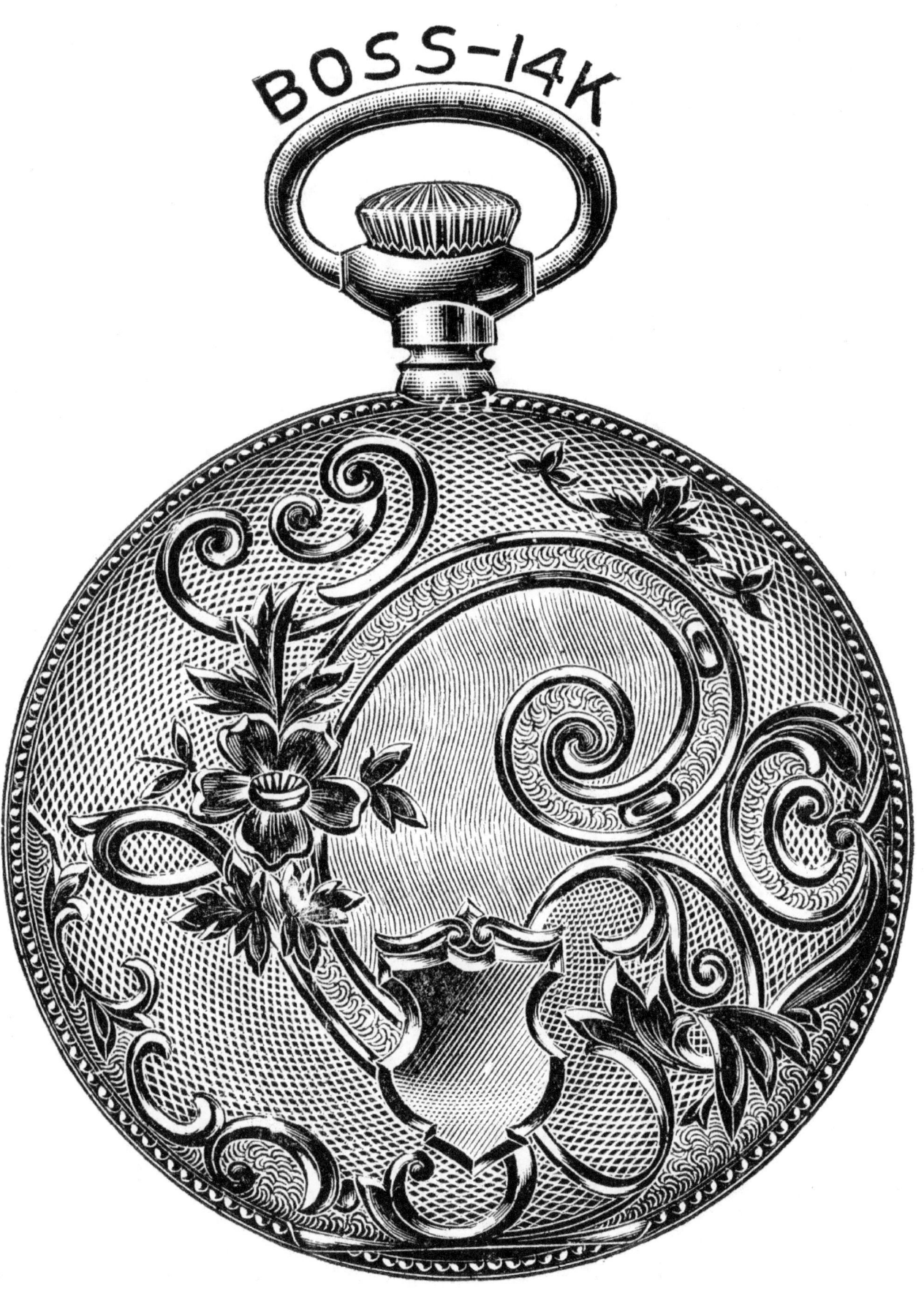

www.ingramcontent.com/pod-product-compliance
Lightning Source LLC
Chambersburg PA
CBHW080709190526
45169CB00006B/2304